# THE LEADERSHIP
# PLAYBOOK

# THE LEADERSHIP
# PLAYBOOK

## STRATEGIES FOR
## SUCCESS IN
## TODAY'S
## WORLD

SUCCESS
BOOKS
Lake Mary, FL

# CONTENTS

# CHAPTER 1

# BECOME THE LEADER OF YOUR OWN LIFE

By Jack Canfield

Leadership isn't just for leaders. In fact, in the ever-evolving pursuit of the lifestyle, career, and assets you want, one of the most transformative shifts you can make is to take a leadership role *in your own life*.

Today, leadership is not just for CEOs, managers, or team captains. Leadership is for anyone who wants to shape their own destiny, make an impact, and inspire others through their actions, even when no official title is given. By embracing a set of core principles that all great leaders understand, you too can take full control over your decisions, your actions, and ultimately your future.

## TAKE 100 PERCENT RESPONSIBILITY FOR YOUR FUTURE

One of the most prevalent myths we often hold is the belief that we're somehow entitled to a fulfilling life—that simply by being on this planet, we deserve happiness, successful careers, enriching relationships, and limitless opportunities. We wait for these things to appear, and when they don't, we place blame—on circumstances, other people, or the world itself.

But one of the most profound truths you must embrace to achieve lasting success is this: There is only one person responsible for the life you're living. That person is *you*.

If you want to be successful, you have to take 100 percent

responsibility for everything you experience in your life—from the level of your achievements to the results you produce, to the quality of your relationships, to the state of your health and physical fitness. Even responsibility for your feelings, your income, your debts—everything!

You have to do those things that will bring you the life that you want. You have to stop blaming—other people, the economy, your boss—for the way things are, and you have to stop complaining about how you wish things were different.

## RESPOND DIFFERENTLY TO GET THE OUTCOMES YOU WANT

One of the tenets I teach in my book *The Success Principles*™ is this equation:

$$E+R=O$$

Event + Response = Outcome

It's a powerful formula that demonstrates that every outcome (O) we get in life is a direct result of our response (R) to the countless events (E) that occur every day. Whether it's a bad economy, workplace politics, an inattentive spouse, government or industry regulations, the city you live in, the fact that you have small children or aging parents to care for—or something else—many of these situations can't be helped. They just are. But if these situations were *the deciding factor* in whether someone was successful or not, no one would ever achieve anything. If we were truly honest with ourselves, we would realize that for every event that stops millions of people from getting what they want, hundreds of other people face that same event and succeed.

What about your own life?

Whether your outcomes have been financial success or financial scarcity, helpful relationships or disconnection, easy workdays or repeated frustration—all of it depends on how you responded to the events that have come up for you.

The good news is that *how you respond* is always your choice.

You can choose to blame the event—or you can take 100 percent responsibility and simply respond differently to it. Once you decide to change your responses, your outcomes will begin to improve. In fact, with this single decision, suddenly you'll begin to act with purpose. When faced with any event, you'll think consciously about your desired outcomes—then control your actions, behaviors, and thoughts so they move you toward success instead of keeping you in victimhood.

> "The indispensable first step to getting the things you want out of life is this: decide what you want."[1]
>
> —BEN STEIN
> WRITER, ACTOR, AND SOCIAL COMMENTATOR

## DECIDE WHAT SUCCESS MEANS TO YOU

Of course, the biggest step toward taking responsibility for your future is to decide what *success* looks like for you.

You must decide what you want.

Unfortunately, most people bungle this crucial first step because they simply can't see how it's possible to get what they want—so they don't even let themselves want it.

But one of the most amazing phenomena you'll ever experience once you decide what you want is the unexpected phone call, the windfall financial benefit, or the uncanny new acquaintance that brings you exactly what you want or need in order to achieve your loftiest goals—almost as if it were planned.

Perhaps it's the universe, rewarding your new decision and take-action attitude by harnessing all the forces at its disposal. Or perhaps you've worked hard and have "grown" yourself to the point where you're finally ready to receive a benefit that had been waiting in the wings all along.

But more probably, as researchers have now come to believe, it may simply be a matter of your subconscious mind focusing on and recognizing opportunity when it arrives.

Whatever the explanation, the reality is that what you want, *wants you.* Your goals, desires, and needs are patiently waiting to gravitate toward you, once you decide what you truly want.

Of course, the main reason that most people don't get what they want is they haven't decided what that *want* is. They haven't defined their goals—exactly—in clear and compelling detail. After all, how else can your mind know where to begin looking, seeing, and hearing if you don't give it specific and detailed goals to achieve?

Instead, take some time to think deeply about what you want in the major areas of life:

**Financial**: Write down your specific financial goals. How much do you want to earn annually? By when do you want to achieve these income levels?

**Career**: Outline your career aspirations. What positions do you want to hold? What milestones do you want to reach, and by when?

**Recreation**: List the hobbies and leisure activities you want to pursue. How often do you want to engage in these activities, and by when?

**Health and fitness:** Specify your health and fitness goals. What weight, fitness level, or lifestyle habits do you aim to achieve, and by when?

**Relationships**: Describe your ideal relationships. What qualities do you seek in your personal and professional relationships? By when do you want to strengthen or build these connections?

**Personal development:** Identify the skills or knowledge you want to acquire. What courses or experiences do you plan to undertake, and by when?

**Community and contribution:** Define your goals for community involvement. What causes do you want to support, how do you want to contribute, and by when?

By writing down your goals in each area, you'll create a comprehensive blueprint for an exceptional future. Not only will this kind of clarity keep you motivated; it will also give you the ultimate road map for achieving your desires.

## EVERY GOOD LEADER STAYS FOCUSED ON RESULTS

Successful people don't always start with lots of money or high-level connections or other privileged circumstances, but they do stay focused on results that matter. They know which achievements will amplify and uplevel their lives, and they stay focused on accomplishing those goals. They research the steps, make plans, take action, and persevere until the results they want are achieved.

### They also stay focused on their core genius.

You have a unique ability or area of brilliance inside of you: something you love to do and do so well it's effortless for you (and a whole lot of fun). If you could make money doing it, you'd make it your lifetime's work.

Successful people believe this too. That's why they take the time to discover their unique brilliance, then put it first as a priority. They focus on it. And they delegate everything else.

Compare that to the rest of the world who go through life doing everything—even those tasks they're bad at or that could be done cheaper, better, and faster by someone else. They can't find the time to focus on their area of brilliance because they fail to delegate even the most menial of tasks.

### Determine what you're brilliant at—then delegate everything else.

To help you determine your area of profound expertise (and those tasks you really should be delegating to others), follow the steps here. Keep in mind that you're looking for the one, two, or three activities—your unique abilities—that not only bring you the most money but also bring you the most enjoyment and that you could spend all day doing.

**Step 1:** Start by listing all those activities that occupy your time, whether they're business-related, personal, or related to your civic organizations or volunteer work. List even small tasks, such as confirmation phone calls or paying bills.

**Step 2:** Choose from your list one to three things *that you are brilliant at*—things that very few other people can do as well as you.

**Step 3:** Next, choose those one to three activities from the previous list *that generate the most income* for you or your company.

**Step 4:** Circle individual activities that you selected in *both* step 2 and step 3. In other words, list activities that you are brilliant at *and* that generate the most income. These are the activities or areas of expertise where you'll want to focus the most time and energy.

**Step 5:** Name any toxic tasks from your original list in step 1 that you especially dislike or that take too much of your time—activities you would gladly delegate to someone else if you could.

**Step 6:** Delegate those toxic tasks and less profitable activities. Find a capable person you trust; then delegate tasks *completely*. Explain the process fully and give 100 percent authority to accomplish the task in the future, rather than delegating it each time it needs to be done.

### Build a team that lets you focus on your core genius.

Every high achiever has a powerful team of key staff members, consultants, vendors, and helpers who do the bulk of the work while he or she is free to create new sources of income and new opportunities for success. The world's greatest philanthropists, athletes, entertainers, professionals, and others also have people who manage projects and handle everyday tasks—enabling them to do more for others, hone their craft, practice their sport, and so on.

If you're a business owner or career professional, start training key people to take over the lesser tasks you identified. If you're a one-person business, start looking for a dynamic number-two person who could handle your projects, book your sales transactions, and completely take over other tasks while you concentrate on what you do best. If philanthropic pursuits or community projects are your business, there are volunteers you can recruit to help you—including college interns, who may work solely for class credit or a good letter of recommendation.

### Build a network based on genuine relationships.

In addition to having a highly trained team, one of the most important skills for success in today's world, especially for entrepreneurs and business owners, is networking. Jim Bunch, the creator of the Ultimate Game of Life, once stated, "Your network will determine your net worth." In my life this has proved to be true. The more time I've spent consciously building and nurturing my network of advisers, colleagues, clients, students, and readers, the more successful I have become.

Businesses and careers are built on relationships, and relationships form when people meet and interact with each other over time in an authentic and caring way. As I'm sure you're aware, statistics confirm over and over that people prefer to do business with people they know, respect, and trust. Nurturing a powerful network will yield results long into the future.

## SET GOALS THAT HELP YOU STAY FOCUSED

Extensive study has shown that once we decide what we want, the brain actually helps us bring about these life-changing results. For instance, experts know that when you give it a goal, the brain triggers its *reticular activating system*—a web of neuro-pathways that filters through the millions of random images, facts, and information we're bombarded with each day, then sends to our conscious mind those bits of data that will help us achieve our goals.

When you give the brain an image of something you want to achieve, it will labor around the clock to find ways to achieve the picture you put there. Without a doubt the brain is a goal-seeking instrument.

> "Focus on doing the right things instead of a bunch of things."[2]
>
> —MIKE KRIEGER
> COFOUNDER OF INSTAGRAM

## HOW MUCH BY WHEN?

Considering that your brain is working for you, it makes sense to be *specific* about the goals you will focus on. When I teach about goal-setting, I stress the importance of setting goals that are both *measurable* and *time-specific*.

**Measurable**—The most powerful goals are those that are *measurable,* both by you and by others. For instance, your goal might be to generate a specific number of new clients for your new consulting firm so you can meet your income goals. By knowing the required number, you can focus on marketing campaigns, referral agreements, and other systems that will hit that number.

**Time-specific**—Your goal should also be *time-specific*. In other words, not only should you state *how much* you'll earn but also *by when* you'll earn it. Only with both these units of measure can you determine whether you've achieved your goal. You also become accountable to meeting your deadline.

Finally, by being so specific, you can focus on the emotions you'll experience when you achieve your goal. Your brain knows the payoff from hitting the target.

### Leaders look for breakthrough goals that can expand their entire lives.

Perhaps the true benefit of any goal is that by pursuing it, you become a more confident, capable person. No one can ever take away the person you become as a result of pursuing your loftiest goals.

In addition to your many weekly and monthly goals, I

recommend that you create *one single goal* such that in the process of achieving it, you expand every aspect of your life—from your finances to your friends, your business success, your lifestyle, and more. Wouldn't that be a goal you would want to work on constantly and pursue with enthusiasm?

I call that a breakthrough goal.

For instance, if you're a consultant and know that you could land big tech companies as clients by speaking at the annual industry conference, wouldn't you work night and day to achieve that goal?

And if you partnered with smaller consulting firms to provide specific services that you can't do yourself, wouldn't that grow your business, your income, and your status in the industry—leading to other opportunities and a far more important network of connections than you have right now?

It would expand everything you do in your career and amplify who you are as a person. That's an example of a breakthrough goal.

---

In closing, to lead your own life successfully, you must embrace responsibility, define what success truly means to you, stay focused on meaningful results, and prioritize your core genius. By also taking 100 percent ownership of your future, you'll ensure that every action and decision moves you closer to your goals. As you step into this role of self-leadership, you'll discover that the life you desire is not only possible but well within your reach.

#### ENDNOTES

1.   "Ben Stein Quotes," Goodreads, accessed April 16, 2025, https://www.goodreads.com/quotes/63051-the-indispensable-first-step-to-getting-the-things-you-want.

2.   "Mike Krieger Quotes," BrainyQuote, accessed April 16, 2025, https://www.brainyquote.com/quotes/mike_krieger_752098.

## About Jack

Known as America's number one success coach, Jack Canfield is the founder and chairman of The Canfield Training Group in Santa Barbara, California, which trains and coaches entrepreneurs, corporate leaders, managers, sales professionals, educators, and the general public in how to accelerate the achievement of their personal, professional, and financial goals.

Jack is best known as the coauthor of the number one *New York Times* best-selling Chicken Soup for the Soul® book series, which has sold more than six hundred million books in forty-nine languages, including forty-one *New York Times* best sellers.

As the CEO of Chicken Soup for the Soul Enterprises, he helped grow the Chicken Soup for the Soul® brand into a virtual empire of books, children's books, audios, videos, CDs, classroom materials, a syndicated column, and a television show, as well as a vigorous program of licensed products that includes everything from clothing and board games to nutraceuticals and a successful line of Chicken Soup for the Pet Lover's Soul® cat and dog foods.

His other books include *The Success Principles™: How to Get from Where You Are to Where You Want to Be* (now available in its 20th Anniversary Edition); *The Success Principles™ Workbook*; *The Success Principles for Teens*; *The Aladdin Factor*; *Dare to Win*; *Heart at Work*; *The Power of Focus: How to Hit Your Business, Personal and Financial Targets with Confidence and Certainty*; *You've Got to Read This Book!*; *Tapping into Ultimate Success*; *Jack Canfield's Key to Living the Law of Attraction*; *The 30-Day Sobriety Solution*; and his recent autobiographical novel, *The Golden Motorcycle Gang: A Story of Transformation*.

Jack is a dynamic speaker and was inducted into the National Speakers Association's Speaker Hall of Fame. He has appeared on more than one thousand radio and television shows, including *The Oprah Winfrey Show*, *The Montel Williams Show*, *Larry King Live*, *The Today Show*, *Fox and Friends*, and two different hour-long *PBS Specials* devoted exclusively to his work. Jack is also a featured teacher in twelve movies, including *The Secret*, *The Meta Secret*, *The Truth*, *The Keeper of the Keys*, *Tapping the Source*, and *The Tapping Solution*. Jack was also honored with a documentary produced about his life and teachings called *The Soul of Success: The Jack Canfield Story.*

Jack has personally helped hundreds of thousands of people on six continents become multimillionaires, business leaders, best-selling authors, leading sales professionals, successful entrepreneurs, and world-class athletes while at the same time creating balanced, fulfilling, and healthy lives.

His corporate clients have included Virgin Records, Sony Pictures, Daimler-Chrysler, Federal Express, GE, Johnson & Johnson, Microsoft, Merrill Lynch, Campbell's Soup, Re/Max, the Million Dollar Forum, the Million Dollar Roundtable, the Young Entrepreneurs' Organization, the Young Presidents' Organization, the Executive Committee, and the World Business Council.

He is the founder of the Transformational Leadership Council and a member of Evolutionary Leaders, two groups devoted to helping create a world that works for everyone.

Jack is a graduate of Harvard, earned his MEd from the University of Massachusetts, and has received three honorary doctorates in psychology and public service. He is married and has three children, two stepchildren, and two grandsons.

For more information, visit www.JackCanfield.com.

# CHAPTER 2

# BREAKING FREE

By J ' X

I was nine years old, enjoying a maiden voyage with my father on a kit boat he'd built when a rogue storm nearly ended our lives.

The air, once calm, became sharp and cold, and dark clouds gathered with unnerving speed as a summer squall caught us in its grip.

We were miles from any human habitation and being tossed around a restless sea. The wind tugged at our sails, and we realized too late that we couldn't lower them. The waves slapped hard against the hull, and water poured into the boat. My father's hands moved frantically as he bailed water with whatever tools he could find. Watching him, I did the only thing I could think of: I took off one of my shoes and started bailing too. It was an act of desperation and an attempt to fight back against forces far greater than ourselves.

But the water kept rising, and I was freezing and soaked. I was alone at one end of the boat, my father at the other, both of us fighting a losing battle.

"This is it," I thought. "My time has come."

But that defeatist thought was immediately followed by a different one. I wanted to live and play and see my mother again. So I did the only thing I could do in that moment. I prayed. I said the Lord's Prayer and spoke from my heart. I promised that if I survived, I would fulfill my purpose, whatever that might be. It was a desperate plea but also a vow—a moment of surrender and resolve.

Then I heard it. Over the chaos of the storm came the hum of an engine. A boat had come to rescue us.

That day was a turning point. Though I didn't realize it at the time, a seed had been planted—the understanding that in moments of crisis, decisions matter—not just any decisions but *directed* ones, decisions that align with what we truly desire for our lives. That moment taught me the power of acting with intention, even when the odds seem insurmountable.

Over the decades, this understanding deepened. Storms are part of life, and each one offers an invitation to decide. Each choice is a step toward the life you'd love to live, a journey of becoming ever more attuned to the director within you—your conscious awareness, the decision-maker that accompanies you into a state of joy and purpose.

You see, there is a way of proceeding through life that acknowledges the profound connection between our focus and our happiness. Imagine that your happiness is like a flower. All flowers are possible. You hold the potential to plant the seeds of growth and fulfillment within the soil of your heart. Every moment of focus is a seed. Every thought, intention, or action is a small seed being sown into the garden of your life. Even during a storm I found myself planting the seed for rescue, for hope, for a way forward. That choice—that focus—became the lifeline that led me through.

This is the essence of resilience: the conscious act of leading yourself out of an unpreferred situation and into a preferred one. The truth is, we are always leading ourselves. Most of the time, however, we do so unconsciously. We drift, letting the currents of our habits, fears, and doubts carry us away from the life we would love. But what if we made it conscious? What if, in every moment, we chose to focus on what we *would* love, to take the smallest step *toward* that vision?

Power lies in the present moment. The present moment is a microgap. It is the sliver of time between the past and the future, between discontent and happiness. This microcrack is always there, waiting for us to notice and use it. It's the space where change begins. Like a flower growing through microcracks in concrete, we have the power to push through, even seemingly under impossible conditions. No matter how much concrete life pours over your dreams, the seeds you plant with intention and care will find a way to grow. They will seek the light, determined, resilient, and unyielding.

As Einstein explained, insanity is doing the same thing and expecting a different result. It's choosing to remain stuck in the concrete, refusing to lead yourself out even when you know that only leads to frustration and regret. But there is a way. You are the leader of your life. It is time to take the reins and say, "I am going to lead myself into a life I love."

This was a challenge I would take up multiple times in my life. When my son was a small child, I collapsed in a restaurant and became paralyzed, trapped in my body and unable to speak. For weeks I languished in the hospital but held an unwavering thought of being at home with my son. I was determined to lead myself out of that hospital and into my own house. To the shock of the doctors, that's exactly what happened, and over time I regained my full ability to walk and speak.

Then, in 2021, I collapsed, unable to move or speak again. The doctors found a brain tumor, told my son to prepare my funeral, and gave me six weeks to live.

That was not going to work for me. That same desire to live that I felt as a nine-year-old girl on a sinking ship was as strong as ever, and eventually, I led my mind to think healing thoughts and led myself home again.

But it wasn't over. Just a few months before this book was published, my body betrayed me again. I woke up and had trouble walking, but I soldiered on. Two days later I couldn't climb the stairs. My son called the ambulance, and by the time they arrived, my speech and movement were impaired. They took me to the hospital, and there I was, in another unpreferred situation.

I wasn't going to give up. I couldn't move, but I could *think*. I began to plant seeds of healing. Just as in 2021, when it was such a treacherous road after returning home still impaired after brain surgery, I was below the concrete again, and I needed to find the microcrack to break through!

When life throws you challenges that seem insurmountable, it's easy to wait—for healing, for help, or for hope. But waiting is passive, and passivity can feel like stagnation.

## THE POWER OF PRESENT GOALS

Sometimes the mountain ahead seems impossible to climb. For me healing from a brain tumor was one of those mountains. At first, even the simplest tasks felt insurmountable. Fatigue plagued me. I would sleep for sometimes thirteen hours straight and then move to a chair, only to fall asleep again, but it never seemed to be enough. I discovered then that the key to moving forward wasn't in tackling the whole mountain at once; it was in focusing solely on what was right in front of me.

In the depths of my struggle I realized that I had to raise my standards. I didn't aim for perfection. I aimed for something that felt just a little beyond my current capabilities. I wanted to be well enough to wash my cup. It was a small goal, but it represented progress—a higher standard of living than I had at the time.

I began with microgoals. First, I set out to wash a single cup. One cup became a few dishes, and eventually, I could clean the entire kitchen. Each step built upon the last, creating a ripple of progress that I could feel and see.

During this journey, I came across a practice used by elite soldiers in high-stress situations. When the stakes are high, they focus solely on the task directly in front of them. This approach resonated deeply with me.

I decided to become my own kind of soldier. My mission was simple: Get the cup from the bedroom, take it to the kitchen, and wash it. That was it. Nothing more, nothing less. By narrowing my focus to one actionable task at a time, I avoided the overwhelm that often accompanies thinking too far ahead.

Each completed task built my confidence.

Progress is born from small, consistent actions. When we focus on what's directly in front of us, we transform impossibility into manageable steps. Over time those steps add up, and the mountain begins to shrink.

Healing taught me that the present moment is where all our power lies. It is a crack in the concrete where we can break through and take deliberate action. When we anchor ourselves in the now, we stop being paralyzed by the enormity of the journey ahead.

In life, as in healing, we can all be soldiers. We can all learn to focus on what's directly in front of us and take the next tiny step. That's how progress happens—one focused, deliberate moment at a time.

## WHERE ALL YOUR POTENTIAL LIES

When life throws you challenges that seem insurmountable, it's easy to wait—for healing, for help, or for hope. But waiting is passive, and passivity can feel like stagnation. Again, I made a decision to stop waiting. I started moving even when my body resisted, even when my hand couldn't rise or my legs felt as if they might give way. I began with qigong and fitness routines, using my functional hand to guide and support the other. Progress felt slow at first, but within weeks I was walking properly again—something that once seemed like a distant dream.

This wasn't magic; it was the power of small, deliberate actions powered by the intention of my heart.

I developed something profound during this decades-long journey: art yoga. At its essence it's a practice of gentle unfolding—a portal between the quantum field of limitless potential and the material world we live in. Rather than being about grand gestures or massive leaps, it's about baby steps.

Every action you take is like planting a seed in the garden of your life. Your heart—your "happy muscle"—is at the center of it all. Much as your physical heart pumps blood, your happiness heart fuels your joy and fulfillment. Happiness is not a random accident; it's a muscle that strengthens with intentional use.

Yoga, which means connection, serves as a metaphor for this work. It teaches us to connect our inner potential with our outer reality. And the key to unlocking this connection is choice. What will you do today to choose happiness, even in a very small, manageable way?

Happiness is like a flower. All flowers are possible, but you must plant the seeds intentionally. During my time in the hospital I didn't plant seeds of despair or resignation. Instead, I envisioned a life where I would return home, where I would be by my window, and where I would one day see my grandson born. Those seeds, nurtured daily, grew into the reality I'm living now.

Had I given up, I wouldn't have experienced the joy of holding my grandson for the first time or basking in the warmth of his smile. This is the beauty of life—it's precious and fleeting, and it's waiting for you to lead yourself from it and out into the world. It is already here in the quantum field, ready for you to grab hold of it.

## What Seeds Will You Plant?

The journey of a life you love starts with the smallest decision in your heart. Every thought and every action is a seed that will grow into the garden of your life.

Are you waiting for healing, happiness, or success to come to you?

What small, deliberate action can you take right now to move closer to your dreams?

How can you strengthen your "happy muscle" by choosing joy, even in what people see as difficult moments?

Your heart is looking for you to love your life. It's calling you to lead yourself with conscious intention rather than on autopilot, ever more experiencing the fulfillment and joy you deserve.

So, what will you do today to take one step closer to the life you've always imagined?

———·———

When I taught architecture, I was teaching something far deeper than design—I was unknowingly teaching the principles of art yoga. Building a home, like building a life, requires more than just materials and blueprints; it requires vision, intention, and a profound understanding of the practice of creation. It's about psychology too, because our bodies are like libraries, recording every event, emotion, and experience we live. And just like a library, we can reformat and reorganize those records. We can rewrite our stories.

The most powerful lesson I've learned is this: You are already leading yourself, whether you realize it or not. But are you leading yourself toward what you truly love, or are you drifting with the current of life's circumstances?

When I was in the hospital, I could have fixated on what I didn't want—the pain, the fear, the uncertainty. Instead, I chose to focus on what I loved: standing at my window, admiring the stars, and holding my grandson. That focus became my compass, guiding me out of darkness and into the life I would love to live.

Here's the truth: Unhappiness, like cold and darkness, is finite. There is a limit to how cold it can get—scientists know this. If you do the research, you will find that absolute zero is the point at which matter stops moving and cannot get colder. Eventually, coldness ends. But heat, like happiness, has no upper limit. The warmth of joy, the fire of hope, and the light of possibility can always grow brighter, warmer, and stronger.

The question is, Will you let it?

Life is a series of ups and downs, of storms and calm seas, of trials and triumphs. From a child bailing water with a shoe in a desperate bid for survival, to being paralyzed, to eventually experiencing a miraculous recovery, I have learned one unshakable truth: We hold the power to lead ourselves, even in the darkest moments.

Rather than waiting for circumstances to change, it's about finding the microcracks, the slivers of possibility, and stepping through with determination and grace.

You don't need to see the entire path ahead. Begin with the smallest step. Plant the smallest seed. The flower shooting forward remains blind to the sunshine above the soil or concrete. Yet in its heart is a happy knowing, a faith that warmth and goodness lie beyond.

In the end it's not the storms that define us but the seeds we plant and the steps we take. Every seed is a spark of growth. Every step is a small crack in the concrete. And with intention and grace, you can lead yourself into the warmth of a life you love.

## About J ' X

As a certified Life Mastery Consultant with the Life Mastery Institute, the premier training center for transformational coaching, J ' X can help you create a life that you absolutely love living.

For over forty-five years J ' X has studied and implemented transformational success principles, acquiring, despite much mental and physical trauma, a wealth of valuable experience through creating works of art, music, literature, and design—as well as mentoring others to tap into their potential and flourish despite their circumstances. As architectural designer in residence at Robert Gordon University, she mentored students both for studio support and for live architectural projects, based on art project community gardens that she devised and ran.

J ' X worked in the prestigious Scottish Design Centre in Glasgow before going freelance.

As an artist she was published by Cannes Down Press and exhibited throughout the UK, including Mandel's in London. She won the social housing Helen McGregor Award and has been a voluntary chair or vice chair of a major housing association continuously for over fifteen years; during that time she was involved in the designing and delivering of an urban village. She has written four books and a play, all focused on supporting and developing the human potential. She shared a stage with Cliff Hague, prior Royal Town Planning Institute president, talking about the importance of planning on people's mental and physical health.

Ever mindful of the environment, J ' X established the first SEPA registered domestic light bulb recycling and battery collection center in the UK, visiting schools to talk about sustainability before sustainability was a thing.

Now J ' X is focused on helping people unfold their inner potential in order to live their dream life. To this end she has developed what she calls art-yoga. Currently she is in the early stages of establishing her Garden of Life project, where the garden acts as a living canvas for art-yoga. It is a place for reconnecting people to nature and each other, a place for sharing and supporting an ongoing legacy of designing and living a life you absolutely love.

J ' X believes that it is never too soon or too late to realize that every circumstance and situation, every strategic conversation is an opportunity to blossom into the life of your dreams.

To learn more about working with J ' X, go to isobydesign.org.

# CHAPTER 3

# THE ALCHEMY OF LEADERSHIP

*Transforming Challenges into Triumphs*

By f. Alexandra Brennan

The sound of screeching tires was the last thing I heard before the car crash. It was a rear-end collision, sudden and jarring, a violent impact of metal on metal that changed the course of my life in an instant.

The pain hit me immediately. As the emergency response team rushed me to the hospital, I became acutely aware that something was terribly wrong. In the emergency room the doctors moved quickly, taking vitals, X-rays, and scans. They reassured me there were no broken bones, no internal bleeding. They told me I was fine and sent me home to follow up with my regular doctor. But my body screamed otherwise. The pain was excruciating, a throbbing pulse that radiated from my neck and head.

Days later a specialist confirmed what my body had been trying to tell me. My C1, atlas bone, had translated off to the left—this is the bone your head sits on! Months later another specialist discovered that the alar ligament, the delicate tissue anchoring my atlas bone—the vertebra that supports my head—had torn. The alar ligament isn't just a piece of anatomy; it's the tether that literally keeps your head on straight.

The fallout was devastating. Severe migraines, vertigo, dizziness, and nausea overtook me every day, and aura migraines compromised my vision, making it impossible to concentrate on my leadership work.

For years I worked as the right-hand and chief of staff for C-level executives, helping to shape solutions for high-powered executives and their boards. I made the decision to launch my own business as a leadership coach, a dream forged from decades of experience and a deep-seated passion for helping others unlock their full potential. Yet here I was, unable to focus or function. My mission seemed to be unraveling before my eyes.

There were days when I wondered if I would ever return to the work I loved. But if there's one thing I knew about myself, it was this: I don't say never. If no one would help me, I would forge a path to healing myself.

What followed was a journey of determination, research, self-leadership, adaptability, and resilience. I discovered a doctor who specialized in precise, nonsurgical adjustments to the neck. His equipment could move my bone back into place, but the damaged ligaments couldn't hold it steady. I needed more.

So I researched more and found a groundbreaking stem cell specialist. His procedure was unconventional, injecting my own stem cells into the damaged ligaments through the back of my throat. It was a leap of faith, but it worked.

At my lowest point I found strength in the most unexpected place—Jack Canfield's *Success Principles*. His words reminded me that the challenges of leadership mirror the challenges of life. As a leader, my greatest test wasn't in boardrooms or presentations but in the battle to rebuild myself. If I couldn't rise from this, how could I guide others to rise? I needed to power up my potential with positive perseverance and *choose* to be resilient, responsible, and accountable for my actions.

We all go through difficult challenges, and if our focus is on the negative, we'll create a negative reality. Positive perseverance is the fusion of hope, grit, and gratitude. Hope is *choosing* to think and act in a way that's positive and constructive in the face of challenging experiences. Grit is *being all in* to create your future leader self. And gratitude is an appreciation for the little things in life that matter.

This was no longer just about healing my body. It was about

proving to myself, and to the leaders I aspired to serve, that even in the face of insurmountable odds, we can find a way forward.

My journey was far from over, but I had taken the first step. And I would come back stronger than ever. After all, it was fractured leadership that inspired me to start my own business.

I had witnessed failures in leadership and management and, after years of research, had determined the root causes of them and the four core principles that could set them right. Now I would use what I learned to rebuild my body, my mind, and my mission.

I would go back to leading leaders feeling more capable and confident than ever. After all, I was now the living, breathing proof of concept!

## REMODEL YOUR FORT

During my time in corporate consulting, I became fascinated with the principles and nuances of leadership. Over the years, I had witnessed the good, the bad, and the ugly leadership and management styles of the C-suites and their boards. Some of what I saw haunted me—bright, capable teams being torn down and disrespected. Important, innovative projects being sidelined by arrogance and the inevitable company culture fallout. It haunted me. Why were we still in such a crisis with leadership? I decided to look for patterns. I researched and validated my findings with my master's thesis and in 2010 started my own leadership education and coaching business called Leadership Design Alchemists. I self-published my book *The Power of Leadership Foundation First: Four Must-Have Principles for Collaborative Advantage*. My mission was to help transform ordinary status-quo leaders into "Effective Extraordinary and Distinctive Leaders from their Leadership Foundation First."

What I've found is that many leaders know what they need to do but lack the *foundation* that supports success: inner leadership mastery!

Sometimes they allowed their ego to override the good of the group. Other times they were kind to a fault, failing to draw on their authority when the moment called for a strong head and a fast decision. Have you ever found it difficult to be yourself *and* play the role others needed you to play?

Think back to a time when you were a child, and picture a space you loved. Perhaps it was your bedroom or a fort you built. Now imagine you've inherited that space. You're happy to return to it but realize that after years of wear it needs major improvements. It's time for an upgrade to remodel and modernize this fort. If your fort was not built on a solid, structurally sound foundation, it could have cracked walls and may even be sinking.

The essential question becomes, How can you remodel and update your leadership with a better blueprint but keep its special character, the things you love and value most?

This kind of question confronts all leaders as we accept responsibility for the future of our leadership, our employees, and the organizations we've inherited. Do we *choose* to live in the old leadership fortress that needs remodeling, or do we take our leadership to the next level and improve it in a positive, constructive manner from its *foundation* first?

I authored *The Power of Leadership Foundation First* (LFF) because I know that many leaders have excellent skills in their "fort," but they were built on quicksand without a constructive foundation.

I chose the metaphor of remodeling to emphasize the need to keep the best of the old leadership and partner it with new leadership in an organized, intelligent, and loving way. We sketch the blueprint in terms of four Integrated, Interlocking Foundation Power Principles that an Effective Distinctive Leader needs for professional and personal success.

Let's think of your leadership now as a four-piece puzzle that must fit together seamlessly.

How one principle works depends on understanding how another fits with it. These four principles help you retain the qualities and characteristics that make you unique while integrating the foundational tools for today's leadership success.

Whether you're leading a team of one thousand or a team of

two, the four principles are the road map to leading successfully and with an eye toward the future!

## PRINCIPLE 1: TRUST AND AUTHENTICITY

Trust is the cornerstone of all meaningful relationships, and leadership is no exception. Without trust, greatness remains unattainable. Genuine connections, productive teams, and lofty achievements all hinge on this principle.

One of the greatest challenges leaders face is the willingness to be vulnerable. They fear that vulnerability translates as weakness and diminishes their authority. Yet the opposite is true. Vulnerability is a strength, not a liability, and being human is what enables leaders to connect with their teams on a deeper level. When leaders dare to be authentic, they invite trust, which fosters collaboration and progress.

Hubert Joly, former Best Buy CEO, exemplifies this through his "human magic" approach. He transformed Best Buy's culture by prioritizing employee feedback, fostering autonomy, and promoting psychological safety. Joly's leadership style, aligning with authenticity, logic, and empathy, significantly improved employee engagement and turned Best Buy from a struggling retailer into a thriving success.

Mary Barra, GM's CEO, demonstrates trust and authenticity through transparency, accountability, and integrity. She openly addressed challenges such as the 2014 ignition-switch recall crisis, taking personal responsibility and implementing safety improvements. Barra's leadership style has transformed GM's culture and positioned it as a leader in electric vehicles.

Both leaders showcase the importance of authenticity. They prioritize transparent communication, ethical decision-making, and empathetic leadership, which are crucial for building trust with employees, stakeholders, and the public.

To lead with trust and authenticity is to believe in the potential of others and in your own values. By doing so, you don't just lead—you inspire, you connect, and you build something far greater than yourself.

## PRINCIPLE 2: EMOTIONAL AND SOCIAL INTELLIGENCE

Leadership that thrives on trust must also be rooted in emotional and social intelligence. This means recognizing what truly matters to your employees, stakeholders, and peers. Social intelligence builds upon this by being genuinely curious about the people around you.

Empathy is the key. It starts with asking meaningful questions and actively listening—not just to the words but to the emotions and intentions behind them. What matters most to your employees and stakeholders? What drives them personally and professionally? What are their goals? When leaders take the time to ask, they create a culture of trust, respect, and shared purpose.

By practicing emotional and social intelligence, leaders create environments where individuals feel seen, heard, and valued.

To lead with emotional and social intelligence is to embrace humanity in all its beautiful complexity. It is the practice of not judging our differences but rather leveraging the diverse points of view into creative and impactful strengths!

## PRINCIPLE 3: SERVING LEADERSHIP

My father, a very wise man and serving leader, once offered me some advice. He told me, "If you want something bad enough, and are passionate enough about it, then you'll do it." At the time, his words frustrated me, but now I see the truth in them. Purpose becomes a mission when it's fueled by passion—a mission bigger than yourself. When you believe in something, it drives you to put in the hard work and serve others selflessly in pursuit of that greater goal.

This principle demonstrates that true leadership is about serving others. Service leadership is following the call to inspire, guide, and uplift those around you and expand your role from one of authority to one of *stewardship, from power over to power with.*

One of the biggest challenges I've witnessed over the years is the pursuing of positions of leadership for the wrong reasons.

They want the title, the salary, and the corner office that come with being "the boss." Those aspirations are not a strong enough foundation to hold things together in challenging times.

If we lead for selfish reasons, the second things get difficult, we start to question if it's even worth it. If we lead in service, however, it's *always* worth it. The mission that drives us forward holds us in place when the boat is rocking in turbulent waters.

When you lead with service, you inspire those around you to do the same. This is the key to creating a *legacy of leadership* that transcends our own ambitions and touches lives in meaningful ways.

## PRINCIPLE 4: CHAOS MANAGEMENT

Most people associate the word *chaos* with fear, destruction, and pandemonium! Yet chaos theory is not the study of things falling apart but rather the study of random and unpredictable behavior.

Imagine how teams and their leaders might respond differently if they redefined chaos altogether.

Chaos—a random and unpredictable situation—is inevitable. Yet the ability to manage chaos effectively is what separates good leaders from great ones. This principle calls for transforming disorder into an opportunity for growth and innovation.

Part of managing chaos begins with understanding that you cannot shoulder it alone. Leaders often feel the need to have all the answers, to rescue their teams with the best ideas, and to be the final voice and vote of any situation. But the true power of leadership lies in collaboration. When faced with chaos, the most effective leaders bring their teams together, leveraging diverse perspectives to create a collective solution.

A common mistake in chaos management is viewing disorder as a negative obstacle to overcome. Instead, innovative leaders should work to shift perspectives, helping their teams see chaos not as a roadblock but as fertile ground for growth and creativity.

To lead through chaos is to embrace the unpredictable and transform it into a source of strength.

## LEADERSHIP: A WAY OF BEING

Leadership is not a title or a position—it's a way of being. Each of the four core power principles offers a vital puzzle piece in your leadership foundation.

These principles are not abstract ideals but values that invite leaders to step into their roles with integrity and purpose. When combined, they enable leaders to balance strength with trust and vulnerability, authority with empathy, and stability with innovation.

My own journey has shown me this truth in ways I could never have anticipated. After the accident, the life I had built and the leadership coaching business that was my passion and purpose seemed to be slipping through my fingers.

But leadership, as I discovered, doesn't happen only in corporations and boardrooms. It happens in the adaptable moments you decide to get back up, push forward, and shift your perspective around any challenge that comes your way.

With intentions of service and authenticity, we can create a future where leadership isn't just a buzzword but a powerful, positive, and constructive catalyst for connection, impact, and growth!

Essential to this process is the daily inner work of leadership—your Innovative Leadership Reinvention and Transformation. This involves deep reflection, honest self-assessment, and surrounding yourself with a mentor or coach who offers unbiased perspectives. By engaging in continual introspection and embracing new mindsets, a future leader vision, and your power principles, you can unlock your full potential and drive meaningful change in your organization and community.

This is why a continual focus on the inner leadership mastery work and your leadership learning journey is so critical now. The world needs Effective Distinctive Leaders. The world needs *you*!

Seize this pivotal moment to reach your true potential—control your Leadership Destiny and Legacy now!

## About Fran

f. Alexandra Brennan, known as Coach Fran, is a transformational leadership coach, alchemist, author, and thought leader revolutionizing twenty-first-century leadership. As the CEO and founder of Leadership Design Alchemists (LDA), she partners with purpose-driven leaders to forge their Leadership Foundation© and Leadership Brand©, catalyzing Effective Distinctive Leadership results and sustainable organizational success.

With a unique blend of corporate experience, academic credentials, and entrepreneurial spirit, Coach Fran has positioned herself as a catalyst for change in innovative reinvented and transformed leadership. Her journey within Fortune 100 and 500 corporations, including Tetley Inc., Cartier Inc., and McKinsey & Co., provided invaluable insights into corporate leadership dynamics, as she worked directly with C-level executives and their boards.

Coach Fran's groundbreaking approach is encapsulated in her book, *The Power of Leadership Foundation First: Four Must-Have Principles for Collaborative Advantage*. This innovative leadership work outlines her 4-Core Integrated Foundation Power Principles© framework, a cornerstone of her transformative methodology:

- Trust/Authenticity
- Emotional/Social Intelligence
- Servant Leadership
- Chaos Management

Through her Inner Leadership Mastery Excellerator™ course, Coach Fran guides leaders to unlock their full potential, fostering leadership innovation and reinvention from the "inside out." Her mission is to transform leaders from status quo to effective distinctive leaders who cultivate high-performing collaborative teams, drive sustainable growth, profits, and create organizations where trust, engagement, loyalty, and retention flourish.

As a design thinker and change agent, Coach Fran challenges the status quo, advocating for Leadership Foundation First and authentic Leadership Brand concepts. Her approach is a potent blend of design thinking, strategic acumen, and cross-industry wisdom, aimed at creating world-class leaders and role models in the US.

Coach Fran's academic background includes bachelor's and master's degrees in business management and a bachelor's degree in liberal arts, where she graduated magna cum laude. Her expertise extends beyond the corporate world, with early career experiences in fitness and holistic wellness, which laid the foundation for her aligned, value-driven approach to leadership.

In her personal life, Coach Fran enjoys quality time with her family and maintains an active lifestyle through exercise. She loves swimming and snow skiing and prioritizes creating new adventures through travel.

Are you ready for Leadership Alchemy to catalyze your extraordinary results with a Triple Advantage: Collaborative, Professional and Personal? Coach Fran is your partner and guide to becoming the effective distinctive leader you've always aspired to be, helping you control your leadership destiny and live your leadership legacy, from your Leadership Foundation First!

# CHAPTER 4

# LEADING FOR CONNECTION, IMPACT, AND CHANGE!

By Nick Nanton

I t's their eyes that haunt me to this day—the hollow gaze of young women who had been kidnapped, trafficked, and stripped of their innocence. Those eyes burned into my memory in 2018, the year I first set foot in Haiti with Operation Underground Railroad. I was there to film the raid and rescue of victims ensnared by a female-run trafficking ring.

This was a follow-up operation. The first operation was a success—at first. The perpetrators were arrested and sent to jail, a fleeting moment of triumph. But Haiti's corruption is a formidable beast, and they bribed their way out, slipping back into the shadows. So I was invited to join the team that was returning to Haiti, determined to see the mission through. This time it wasn't just about putting these people back behind bars. We knew there were kids who needed to be rescued—more souls who had been swallowed by the darkness.

Each operation added another layer of anguish to my heart. After Haiti my next trip was to Colombia to document follow-up operations there. Through my team and others we captured the raw moments of liberation and the suffocating aftermath of trauma. Then came Iraq, Mexico, and other places, other missions the memories of which still claw at the edges of my mind.

After one of these trips I was back home, a parent at school sports games. My world had shifted violently between extremes: the sinister depths of human depravity abroad and the seemingly idyllic normalcy of suburban America. People often asked about my trips. Their reactions were predictable—shock and pity for the tragedies unfolding "in other countries." It was a convenient narrative, one that kept the horrors at arm's length.

I bit my tongue at first, but the frustration built until it spilled over one day. Someone remarked how awful it was "over there," and I shot back. "You don't understand," I said. "It's happening *right here.*"

That moment became the seed for my next documentary. Its title: *It's Happening Right Here.* This project exposed the grim reality that human trafficking isn't confined to the dark alleys of impoverished nations. It's in our communities, our backyards, lurking behind the polished facades of gated communities in the United States. The epidemic has woven itself through mediums such as Instagram and TikTok and into our children's bedrooms, and I felt an unshakable responsibility to bring it to light.

The film was more than just a project; it was a mission. It was a lifeline for the voiceless, a battle cry against apathy, and a plea for awareness. As I pieced together stories and footage, I realized that the haunting eyes of those children weren't just a reminder of past operations. They were a call to action—a relentless demand that I keep fighting, keep filming, and keep shouting the truth until the world could no longer look away.

You see, for me, leadership isn't a title. It's not a corner office or a place at the top of the organizational chart. For me, leadership isn't about being a manager but rather being a channel—a channel for connections, for conversations, and for change.

## LEADING BY EXAMPLE

In 1914 explorer Ernest Shackleton embarked on the *Endurance* expedition to cross Antarctica. When his ship became trapped in ice, Shackleton faced a dire situation: twenty-seven men stranded in the harshest environment on Earth.

Shackleton's leadership goal needed to shift. Instead of focusing solely on the expedition's original goal, he shifted his priorities to the survival and morale of his team. He refused to dwell on their misfortune and instead celebrated small victories, such as securing fresh water or hunting seals. He played games, told stories, and distributed responsibilities based on strengths rather than ranks. Shackleton's emotional intelligence fostered unity and resilience.

After two years Shackleton led a daring journey across treacherous waters in a lifeboat to secure help. Every crew member survived, a testament to his extraordinary ability to lead with adaptability, empathy, and an unshakable commitment to his team.

For over a decade I've had the chance to work alongside my good friend, motivational speaker, and veteran Keni Thomas. You might not know who Keni is, but you've likely heard his story.

On October 3, 1993, US forces were deployed into Mogadishu, Somalia, to seize two high-profile officials.

Things went terribly wrong.

A team of Somali militiamen armed with AK-47s and RPG-7s stormed the mission, causing massive bloodshed and bringing US choppers crashing to the ground.

It took the lives of nineteen American soldiers, and more than one thousand Somalis were killed.

But soldier Keni Thomas survived and went on to consult in the making of one of the greatest war movies of all time based on this operation.

That movie was the award-winning *Black Hawk Down*.

Keni's story is one of strength, grit, purpose, and leadership.

When we were in the field working together on a documentary about Keni's leadership academy—where people like you and me learn to "shoot, move, and communicate so we can be better leaders in business and life"—Keni told me the best definition of *leadership* that I've ever heard. Keni said to me, "Nick, leadership is the example you set for the people you serve."

True leadership isn't about pulling rank or exerting authority. It's about who you become when the stakes are high—the kind of person whose energy inspires others. Shackleton's ability to foster hope in the face of despair, Keni's relentless drive to find purpose through adversity—these stories underscore the essence of leadership.

For me, it's about showing up as the person God calls me to be. I am far from perfect, but I strive to lead with kindness and humility, knowing that my actions speak louder than words. I try to model a commitment to continual learning, so those around me are encouraged to grow as well. By being a channel for positivity and purpose, I hope to inspire others to rise above challenges and become leaders in their own right.

## Leading to Connection

Leadership is also about connection. Like many of you, I usually roll my eyes at the thought of networking events, dismissing them as opportunities for people to climb the social or professional ladder. There is a cheapened connotation to the idea of networking because it is often self-serving. Over time, though, I redefined what connection and building a network meant to me. People are a resource—not just for personal gain but as part of a loop of generosity and impact. You call on them for help, support, or resources, and you offer the same in return. It's a cycle that creates momentum for change.

Part of being a leader for me is being a conduit—a connection between stories, people, and resources. Leadership doesn't always mean leading people directly; sometimes it means putting others in touch with what they need to thrive. I've seen this play out in powerful ways. For example, I've worked for many years with Dick Vitale, the legendary ESPN commentator. Dick is relentless in his mission to raise money for childhood cancer research. When he himself was diagnosed with cancer, his drive only intensified. One day he asked me to help him. I told him to make me a video, and I sent it to Mark Cuban. Putting the two of them in each other's orbit resulted in a $500,000 donation from Mark.

Another example is the profound impact of connecting veterans to resources through the *K9s for Warriors* documentary.

After its release I received letters from veterans who credited the program with saving their lives. They had been on the brink of suicide, but the companionship of a service dog and the support of the program gave them a reason to keep going. Those letters are a reminder that leadership is often about being a resource to connect others with what can help them heal, grow, or succeed.

At its core it's about facilitating relationships and opportunities and making introductions that lead to change. Whether it's raising funds for cancer research, saving lives through veteran programs, or simply connecting people who can create magic together, leadership is about building bridges for a greater cause.

I couldn't do what I do in isolation. I am extremely grateful for the experiences I've had and the impact we've made through our books and documentaries, but they were possible only because of the connections we've forged with others. When we come together for a shared purpose, I lead you, you lead me, and together we lead a mission for change.

## LEADING WITH INTEGRITY

A couple of years ago I was introduced to an amazing woman named Brisa De Angulo Losada and asked if I could tell her story. I was ready for that challenge, she agreed, and together we made the documentary *Brisa*.

The film chronicles Brisa's incredible journey. A survivor of childhood sexual violence, Brisa took her fight for justice to the highest legal levels after the Bolivian legal system failed her. She attended Rutgers Law School, became her own lawyer, and ultimately secured a landmark ruling in 2023 that changed the way Latin American countries prosecute cases of violence against children.

When the documentary was complete, we submitted it to the International Documentary Association, the leading organization in the world for documentary filmmakers. It hosts awards every year, and to our amazement *Brisa* landed on its short list for featured documentaries. It picked twenty out of more than seven hundred submissions, and this year four out of five Oscar nominees are from that short list. It was surreal.

But here's the kicker: We got rejected from Sundance, South by Southwest, and countless other organizations. An award consultant asked us where we had screened the film, and we said, "Nowhere." She couldn't believe it. In fact, we were so used to getting rejection letters that we almost deleted the email from the documentary association. Those rejection letters all said the same thing: "You made an amazing film, but we can't screen it." It's hard not to tie your identity to your work when that happens.

Yet part of being a leader is having the ability to lead yourself irrespective of the outcome. It's about showing up with passion, purpose, and perseverance, even when no one is patting you on the back for it.

Ray Dalio's book *Principles* talks about how we often think life is about winning and achieving. When someone asks about your biggest goal, you might say, "I want to win Song of the Year at the Grammys," or something equally ambitious. But Dalio points out that if you set out to achieve that goal and won the next week, it wouldn't mean as much. The easier it comes, the less you respect it. He says the purpose of life isn't winning—it's the good struggle.

The *good* struggle is what gives meaning to the journey. It's about struggling enough to respect the win, cultivating gratitude and appreciation along the way. Most importantly, it's about remembering that your worth isn't tied to the outcome. It's tied to the integrity and perseverance you show as you navigate the highs and lows. That's what makes leadership—and life—truly worthwhile.

## LEADERSHIP: A DECISION TO RISE!

Leadership is not about the titles you hold, the followers you accumulate, or the likes you rack up on Instagram. It's not measured by the number of people who look up to you or the accolades you achieve. Instead, true leadership is about the unseen moments—the choices you make when no one is watching, the connections you forge for the greater good, and the courage to step forward when the path is uncertain. It's about who you become in the process, the integrity you maintain, and the perseverance you embody in the face of rejection, failure, or doubt.

As you read these stories, my hope is that you recognize leadership is not reserved for the extraordinary or the well-known. It's something each of us can embody in our own way, every day. Maybe it's showing kindness when it's easier to be indifferent. Maybe it's bridging the gap for someone in need or standing firm in your values when the world seems to demand compromise. Leadership is a choice—a decision to rise, to serve, and to inspire, even when the outcome is uncertain.

So, as you go forward in your own journey, ask yourself what kind of leader you will be. Will you chase applause, or will you choose purpose? Will you wait for the perfect moment, or will you lead where you stand, with what you have?

Remember, leadership isn't about perfection—it's about persistence. It's about the struggle that shapes you and the legacy of impact you leave behind. Let that be your guiding light, because the world doesn't need perfect leaders. It needs courageous ones.

## About Nick

From the slums of Port-au-Prince, Haiti, with special forces raiding a sex trafficking ring and freeing children, to the Virgin Galactic Space Port in Mojave with Sir Richard Branson, twenty-two-time Emmy Award–winning Director-Producer Nick Nanton has become known for telling stories that connect. Why? Because he focuses on the most fascinating subject in the world: *people*. As an award-winning song-writer, storyteller, and best-selling author, Nick has shared his message with millions of people through his documentaries, speeches, blogs, lectures, songs, and best-selling books. Nick's book *StorySelling* hit The Wall Street Journal Best-Seller List and is available on Audible as an audio-book. Nick has directed more than sixty documentaries and a sold-out Broadway Show (garnering forty-three Emmy nominations in multiple regions and twenty-two wins), including:

- *DICKIE V* (ESPN/Disney+)
- *Rudy Ruettiger: The Walk On* (Amazon Prime)
- *The Rebound* (Netflix)
- *Operation Toussaint* (Amazon Prime)

Nick has shared the stage with, coauthored books with, and made films featuring:

- Larry King
- Kathie Lee Gifford
- Hoda Kotb
- Dick Vitale
- Kenny Chesney
- Magic Johnson
- Coach Mike Krzyzewski
- Jack Nicklaus
- Tony Robbins
- Lisa Nichols
- Peter Diamandis
- And many more

Nick specializes in bringing the element of human connection to every viewer, no matter the subject. He is currently directing and hosting the series *In Case You Didn't Know* (season 1 executive produced by Larry King), featuring legends in the worlds of business, entrepreneurship, personal development, technology, and sports.

Nick's first love has always been music. He has been writing songs for more than two decades, and his songs have been aired on radio across the

United States and in Canada. He is currently ranked in the top 10 percent of songwriters in the world. His songs have been recorded by Lee Brice, Darius Rucker, RaeLynn, Joe Bryson, and many more, and have amassed more than three million streams on Spotify, Apple Music, Pandora, and SoundCloud. He received three Gold records in 2018 for his work with the global touring band A Day to Remember.

Nick has written and/or produced songs that have appeared on the following shows or in promotional commercials for:

- the Fox prime-time series *Glee, New Girl, House*, and *Hell's Kitchen*
- the MLB All-Star Game
- ABC Family's hit series *Falcon Beach*
- the CBS prime-time series *Ghost Whisperer* starring Jennifer Love Hewitt

# CHAPTER 5

# TRANSFORMING VISION INTO REALITY

*A Leadership Journey*

By Joe White

I n 2008 I found myself standing at a crossroads.

After years in the mortgage industry, I couldn't shake the feeling that something was missing. I had met countless aspiring agents who brimmed with ambition but struggled to break through. The problem wasn't their drive—it was the lack of meaningful, practical training. I realized that the industry needed more than just certification courses. It needed a complete overhaul of how we prepared future professionals.

I'd been in the mortgage-brokering industry since 1988 and had started teaching at Seneca College, in the Financial Services Post Diploma Program. I eventually became the program coordinator, responsible for the oversight of that fourteen-course program.

I would watch some of my students who had done extremely well in our training program struggle in the real world.

What I realized is that they were leaving with technical knowledge but had no clue how to actually build a business or structure their lives around it.

They didn't know how to set goals and projections. They didn't know how to differentiate themselves in the market or build affiliate partnerships. They didn't know how to balance the hustle of getting clients with the juggling of family life.

I realized during a particularly frustrating moment that my purpose was to change that and provide for them a road map for success well beyond the classroom and encourage each of them to become CEO of their own lives.

So one late evening, sitting at my desk with notes from numerous conversations scattered around me, a phrase took shape in my mind: "Transforming students into successful entrepreneurs." It wasn't just a tagline. It was a mission—a call to action that would become the foundation of the Real Estate and Mortgage Institute of Canada (REMIC), the company that I founded in 2008. My vision was clear: create an institution that went beyond certifying mortgage agents and actually equipped them with the mindset, skills, and confidence to thrive.

Have you ever felt that pull—the spark of an idea that won't let you go? The kind that keeps you awake at night because you know deep down it's your calling? That's where it all begins.

But an idea alone isn't enough. The idea needs oxygen. It needs action. It needs you to take a stand for it!

## BUILDING A FOUNDATION

Launching a business is like planting a seed. It takes care, patience, and the right conditions to grow. In the early days REMIC was little more than an idea fueled by determination and late nights, working in my unfinished basement. The first challenge was convincing the industry that our approach was different. Licensing courses weren't new, but I knew they could be better. *Much* better.

Instead of outsourcing textbooks or relying on dense, jargon-filled manuals, I decided to write my own. This wasn't just about creating content; it was about reimagining how we taught aspiring agents. I wanted the material to be engaging, practical, and empowering, something I would want to read myself! Drawing from my own experiences, I filled the textbook with real-world scenarios and actionable insights. The goal was simple: prepare students not just to pass exams but to excel in their careers.

I spent an intense three months writing from the morning until the wee hours of the night, focusing on making a difference. But as I came to learn over the years, leadership is a marathon, not a sprint. Early in my journey I made the mistake of believing that *hustle* meant sacrificing everything else. After much trial and error, and yes, many mistakes, including a failed marriage, I realized that true success includes balance. I began implementing simple but effective strategies: structured morning routines, non-negotiable family time, and delegating effectively. A burned-out leader can't inspire anyone. Sustainable leadership is about knowing when to push forward and when to recharge.

Think about the foundations in your life—whether it's your career, relationships, or personal growth. Are they strong enough to support the vision you're building? If not, what needs to change? And how can you be the catalyst for that change?

Like building a house, the strength of your foundation determines the stability of everything that follows.

But a great textbook wasn't enough. I knew we needed a culture of mentorship and community. REMIC wasn't going to be just another training provider; it was going to be a place where students felt supported and inspired to reach their full potential. And we wanted to go *big*.

## SCALING THE VISION

There was a moment in REMIC's early days when I questioned if we could compete with established licensing institutions. Industry insiders told me our model was "too ambitious." But instead of backing down, I doubled down. I reached out to students and asked them directly what they needed. I contacted those whom I'd taught at Seneca who were now becoming leaders themselves and asked them what *they* needed. That moment reshaped our approach—it wasn't about competing; it was about serving our students and the industry better than anyone else.

As REMIC began to gain traction, I quickly realized that growth came with its own set of challenges. Leadership became more than just managing operations—it was about setting a standard. I made it a point to lead by example. Whether it was staying late to mentor students, stepping into the classroom to teach, or ensuring every instructor met the highest standards, I wanted to show that excellence wasn't negotiable.

This hands-on approach paid off. Over time REMIC grew to command 75 percent of the market share in mortgage licensing education. But for me, success wasn't about market dominance—it was about *impact*. Each student who walked out of our doors confident and ready to succeed was a testament to the vision we had set in motion.

Building a great team was another cornerstone of our success. I didn't just hire employees; I cultivated a culture. Inclusivity, camaraderie, and shared purpose became its pillars. One of the most memorable milestones was a weeklong company retreat in Mexico. It wasn't just about celebrating success; it was about strengthening bonds and reaffirming our shared mission.

Our team's culture is one of helping, whenever and wherever we can. We partnered with an orphanage for children of violence in Mexico, supporting its mission to change their lives. We brought supplies to that orphanage on this trip, visited with the children, and saw the impact that our support provided.

One of the most rewarding aspects of leadership is watching people grow into their potential. I remember a team member who joined REMIC at an entry-level position, unsure of his abilities. Over time, through mentorship and encouragement, he developed confidence and eventually stepped into a leadership role. Watching his transformation reinforced my belief that great leaders don't just manage—they elevate those around them.

What about your team? Whether it's in your workplace, your community, or your personal circle, are you fostering an environment where people feel valued and inspired? How can you set the standard for the kind of culture you want to see?

Scaling isn't just about profit. It's about building a culture that stands the test of time, can foster and hold growth, and is inspiring enough to attract both top talent and eager clients.

## BREAKING NEW GROUND

Leadership requires the courage to embrace change and innovate.

With REMIC firmly established as a leader in mortgage education, I began to see other opportunities for transformation. The life-insurance sector, much like mortgages, was bogged down by outdated training and uninspired teaching methods. I realized that our student-first approach could make a difference there too.

Expanding into life-insurance licensing courses was a natural next step. We applied the same principles that had made us successful in mortgages: practical training, real-world scenarios, and a focus on empowering students. The results spoke for themselves. Our mission of "transforming students into successful entrepreneurs" was no longer confined to one industry—it was shaping careers across sectors.

As we move into a digital-first world, education is evolving faster than ever. The next frontier of professional development will integrate AI-driven personalized learning experiences. At REMIC we are already exploring adaptive learning technologies that tailor coursework to individual strengths and weaknesses, ensuring that every student receives a uniquely effective education. The leaders of tomorrow must be ready to embrace these advancements.

Consider your own journey. Are there areas in your life or work where you've settled for "good enough" when you could be striving for excellence? Sometimes breaking new ground means stepping out of your comfort zone and taking a risk on something you truly believe in.

## RECOGNITION AND LEGACY

Leadership isn't about seeking accolades, yet recognition has a way of finding those who lead with purpose.

In 2019 I was inducted into the Canadian Mortgage Hall of Fame—an honor that reaffirmed the impact REMIC had made on the industry. A few years later, in 2024, REMIC was named

Industry Service Provider of the Year, further solidifying our reputation as a leader in professional education.

But for me, the most meaningful recognition comes from our students. Over nineteen hundred five-star Google reviews paint a picture of an institution that doesn't just educate but empowers. Each review is a reminder of why we started this journey and why we continue to push forward. And I respond to each and every review personally.

What about your legacy? When the dust settles, how do you want to be remembered? For me, leadership isn't about titles or trophies—it's about the lives you've touched and the impact you've made. Determining the legacy you want to leave is one of the most profound exercises in self-reflection. To do that, you must ask yourself some essential questions and take deliberate steps toward shaping the story you want others to tell.

Start by considering your core values. These are the principles that guide your decisions even when the pressure to compromise is high. Are you driven by integrity, creativity, service, or something else entirely? Your legacy should reflect these values, acting as a testament to what mattered most to you.

Next, think about the people in your life—the family, colleagues, and community members you influence daily. What kind of mark do you want to leave on them? Leadership isn't just about professional achievements; it's about how you inspire those around you. What do you want others to remember most about their interactions with you?

Another powerful way to explore your legacy is to identify the problems you want to solve. Every industry faces challenges. What issues resonate with you? Focusing on a cause that matters to you adds depth and direction to your legacy.

Pause for a moment and answer this question: If someone were to summarize your life in one sentence, what would you want that sentence to be? It's a sobering question, but it can reveal the essence of the legacy you want to build. This vision can act as a compass, guiding your decisions so that your actions align with the story you want your life to tell.

Remember, shaping your legacy isn't just about monumental achievements; it's also about how you show up in the everyday moments. The way you treat people—your kindness, your honesty, your willingness to listen—will leave a lasting impression. Each interaction is an opportunity to reinforce the values you want others to associate with you.

As you move forward, recognize that your legacy isn't static. It can and should evolve as you grow. What matters to us in our twenties may not hold the same weight twenty years later!

In the end the legacy you leave isn't about wealth or accolades; it's about the lives you've touched and the principles you stood for. By leading with purpose, investing in people, and staying true to your values, you can leave a legacy that resonates for decades to come. And that is a life well-lived.

## The Future of Leadership

As REMIC continues to grow, my role as a leader evolves along with it. Leadership, I've learned, is about more than steering a company. It's about inspiring people to see their potential and giving them the tools to realize it. Whether it's refining course materials, mentoring instructors, or ensuring our culture remains intact, my focus remains on service.

I firmly believe in lifelong learning as well. I instituted a program whereby my staff can take any course they want, from any institution, college, or university, and REMIC pays for it. I take several courses a year to improve my knowledge in my field and learn how to identify opportunities that I may not be aware of. And I can tell you that learning has paid off and continues to do so. I feel I'm a better leader and person because of it.

Great leaders don't just build companies; they build people. They create environments where individuals feel valued, supported, and empowered to succeed. That's the legacy I strive to leave—not just for REMIC but for every student and team member who becomes part of our story.

What kind of leader do you want to be? Are you empowering those around you to reach their potential, or are you simply managing tasks? True leadership starts with a vision but thrives through service and action.

## LESSONS IN LEADERSHIP

Reflecting on my journey, a few key lessons stand out:

1. **Lead with purpose:** A clear mission creates a lasting impact. When your vision is driven by purpose, it inspires others to follow.

2. **Invest in people:** Building a strong team culture fosters growth and loyalty. Success isn't a solo endeavor—it's a team sport.

3. **Adapt and innovate:** Staying ahead of industry trends ensures longevity. Innovation isn't optional; it's essential.

4. **Lead by example:** Actions speak louder than words. Set the standard you want others to follow.

5. **Celebrate success together:** Recognition and team building strengthen an organization. Success is sweeter when it's shared.

Your leadership journey can start today. Whether you're leading a company, a small team, or just yourself, remember, true leadership is about vision, service, and impact. Set bold goals. Lift others as you rise. And never stop learning. After all, the best leaders don't just create success—they create a legacy that lasts beyond them.

## About Joe

Joe White, a visionary leader and best-selling author, has devoted thirty-five years to empowering entrepreneurs in the financial services sector. As a celebrated educator and trainer, Joe's profound influence is reflected in the success of over sixty thousand copies of his books sold worldwide, each designed to enhance the potential of aspiring business leaders.

As the founder, president, and CEO of the Real Estate and Mortgage Institute of Canada (REMIC), Joe has shaped industry standards since 2008, building on his significant experience as the former head of the mortgage broker program at Ontario's largest college. His expertise and leadership were formally recognized in 2019 when he was inducted into the Canadian Mortgage Hall of Fame, a testament to his impact and dedication to the field.

Furthering his commitment to integrity and excellence, Joe established the Association of Mortgage Investment Professionals (AMIPROS) and the Fraud Prevention Centre of Canada (FPCC). These organizations underscore his dedication to nurturing a thriving environment for professionals and championing national efforts in fraud prevention and awareness.

In 2024 Joe launched *The Billion Dollar Podcast*, a dynamic platform where he shares innovative strategies that transcend industry boundaries, helping individuals achieve remarkable success and make a significant impact on their communities and beyond.

Residing in the Greater Toronto area with his family, Joe continues to inspire change and drive progress within the financial sector. He is accessible for further insights and collaboration via email at joe.white@remic.ca.

# CHAPTER 6

# THE JOURNEY OF BECOMING A LEADER

By Bob Kawabe

Tears stung in my eyes as the weight of my cousin's words hit me like a ton of bricks.

"Don't call her mom," she said, "She's not your mother."

Just a few minutes earlier, I was a carefree six-year-old, running around the neighborhood with no curfew, restrictions, or worries.

She snapped me back to my harsh reality.

You see, as a child, I didn't know what it meant to have a family. I never lived with my mother and spent my earliest years bouncing between relatives and strangers—people who got paid to care for me but never truly my own family.

After living with a stranger who initially took care of me, at six years old I was sent to stay with my aunt. She took care of my basic needs, but I was essentially on my own, and I was fearless. I ran around with kids twice my age, carrying a chip on my shoulder big enough to block the sun. I had no one to tell me what I could or couldn't do, and I wore that independence like armor. I could stay out as late as I wanted, take risks other kids wouldn't dare, and live without fear.

But independence isn't a substitute for belonging. I realized that the night my cousin shattered my illusion. I had called my aunt "Mom" and was immediately reminded that she was not my mom.

That night, I cried myself to sleep, saying, "I don't belong here." My heart felt empty. I only saw my mom a handful of times over my first ten years of life, but finally, she came for me. I was ecstatic!

I now had a real mom and an instant family that included a stepfather and a younger brother. My heart was full of hope, but it was short-lived.

My new family came with rules and restrictions I couldn't understand. I had always been a free and active child, and suddenly, I couldn't go outside. I couldn't play sports. I began to hear the phrases "No" and "You cannot" regularly. If I questioned anything, I was punished. I was constantly isolated and grounded and felt like a caged bird, my sense of self diminishing with every passing year. After a while, it was almost as though I developed a split personality. At home I became someone else: quiet, obedient, walking on eggshells to avoid conflict. But outside I was wild. I got into trouble, accepted every dare, and chased every thrill. All the frustration of being caged spilled out like a flood.

The family I thought would complete me did not turn out as I had hoped for. At home I felt like a shadow of myself and struggled to process the fact that even here with my own mom I still didn't belong.

Several years later, during the summer before my junior year, my mom took me to Southern California, and it was there that I found freedom again. Hitchhiking up the Coast from LA to San Francisco, surfing every day, and playing lots of basketball, I rediscovered who I was.

Looking back, I realize that sometimes it's the emptiness that teaches us who we are. Losing my freedom and regaining it made me appreciate freedom that much more and helped to confirm who I truly was.

Life teaches through contrast. The heartache and struggles shape us. And through it all I learned to stay true to myself and not let anyone define who I am.

Coach John Wooden said, "Be true to yourself. Be true to those you lead."[1]

That summer before my junior year reconnected me to the identity I had lost. That taste of freedom reminded me of my essence, the sense of agency I craved, and I knew I could never go back.

When I returned to Hawaii for my senior year, I decided to live on my own, and I've been on my own ever since.

That shift in my life, that fight for my sovereignty, shaped who I am and how I choose to serve. Today I am the founder of Kawabe Advisory Group, and we created this company with a single mission in mind: To touch the lives of others by giving hope, helping to define purpose, and inspiring people to realize their dreams.

We help people live their "Amazing Life of Significance" so they can spend time with those they care about and love, doing what they are passionate about and making an impact on the lives of others. Business and financial success are just the tools. They do not define our purpose for why we are here. My goal is to help people reconnect to their hearts, their purpose to live, and experience the self-fulfillment no amount of money can buy.

I learned that risking it all to protect your sense of self is a risk worth taking. In fact, the concept of risk is foreign to me. I see everything I do as an *opportunity* rather than a risk, and this perception has led me to numerous breakthroughs in my life.

On the professional level I've worked on full commission from day one. Some might see that as a risk. I saw it and still see it as an opportunity to be in control of my own destiny. The only limits are the ones I impose on myself. It's up to me to make things happen. How great is that? It is very empowering!

And it has shaped the principles by which I live my life, both personally and in business.

## TRUST YOURSELF

The memory of opening the refrigerator door only to find it empty was the turning point of my life. I had just graduated high school and had no food or job and just twenty dollars left to my name. Rent was due in two weeks, and I needed an income—immediately!

I walked for blocks, knocking on every door, but no one would hire me. I'd hear the same thing over and over: *"You don't have experience.*" And I kept thinking, *"How can I get experience if no one hires me?"*

But I didn't let that stop me. I just knew I would find the way. In Hawai'i, there's something called a pedicab—a bike with seats that tourists ride in, like a rickshaw. It wasn't glamorous, but I didn't care. For forty dollars a week I rented that bike and worked twelve-hour shifts pedaling tourists around at night, and I surfed during the day. It wasn't easy, but it worked. I earned enough to pay my rent, fill my fridge, and keep going.

From there other opportunities came. I worked on cruise ships as a waiter and even became a flight attendant for a while. Each step forward was a reminder: I could solve my problems because I trusted myself to find a way and because my mission mattered to me.

That mission was twofold: to have my autonomy and to prove to myself that I could be successful on my own.

You might face moments when the odds feel stacked against you and doors slam in your face, but in those moments, remember this: The solution isn't outside of you; it is all within you! We control our own destiny by trusting our ability to figure things out. When it seems everything is going against you, remember this: It is up to us to keep pushing forward and make it happen, because no one is going to do it for us!

We have got to have a bright vision of our future and believe that anything in life is possible and do whatever it takes to live the life we want to live!

## SHIFTING YOUR MINDSET

When I landed my first professional job selling copiers, it was 100 percent commission-based—no salary, no safety net. Success meant knocking on thousands of doors, most of which slammed shut in my face. Over my career I made more than twenty thousand cold calls, practically everyone telling me no. It was tough!

But I never saw those noes as rejection. They were stepping stones. Each one brought me closer to a yes!

I turned the grind into a game. I didn't even acknowledge a no as a rejection. I just locked my sights on what I wanted to achieve. The secret? Shifting of the mindset. To me, every obstacle was just an inevitable part of the road to success.

This mindset became a cornerstone of my life, especially in a pivotal moment when I took on a new kind of leadership: coaching my daughter's soccer team and later my sons' team.

Standing in front of those young girls, I saw their trust, their openness, and something even more profound: their untapped potential.

I approached coaching the way I approached life—by leading through action. True leadership means setting an example. Even at my current age, I still push myself to stay fit and practice what I preach, because I believe this: Your mind has the power to break through and push beyond what your body is capable of.

As I coached those girls, I pushed them hard because I wanted to show them what they were capable of. I didn't let them quit or settle for "good enough," and something extraordinary happened.

They broke through. Their mindset shifted. They started believing in themselves. They stopped holding back and started chasing big dreams. Watching them transform was one of the most rewarding experiences of my life.

Here's the lesson I want you to carry with you: Your mindset determines your outcome and reality. Life will challenge you. People will doubt you. Sometimes you may doubt yourself. But that is what fuels us. Shift your perspective, and you'll discover that every setback is an opportunity to grow, to learn, and to rise higher.

When you shift your perspective, you change everything, even rejection. And when you change your mindset, you change your world.

## Your Heart and Passion

When you follow your heart and do what you love and what you are truly passionate about, you are now living your life's purpose. The entire experience changes from the excitement you feel to the energy and the drive you get, because you are living your passion! This feeling is like no other. You just feel unstoppable!

To be the best you can be in everything you do, just follow your heart and know why you are passionate about it. My purpose and passion in life is making an impact on the lives of others, starting with my family. I want to help others have the belief in themselves and know anything in life is possible. They just have to know what they want, have the burning desire to succeed, and do whatever it takes to make it happen!

True success is about giving our very best effort in all we do, and it is never about winning. Winning is a result, which we cannot control, but we have full control over our efforts. Our mindsets give us the positive focus, and our purposes are what fuel our hearts to take action.

For years I operated from a "can do" mindset, and it worked. I was "successful" with what I was doing, but when I began to lead from my heart with purpose, everything changed.

This shift came to life when I started coaching. I wasn't just teaching the kids soccer; I was teaching them life skills, work ethics, and building self-confidence. I never focused on winning or losing. Instead, I taught them the principles of success: effort, discipline, and resilience.

For over twenty years I've had the privilege of coaching athletes, young adults, and business leaders. Those experiences are how I learned success isn't about results; it's about the character you demonstrate during the process.

Coach John Wooden, one of the greatest coaches in history, taught me this invaluable lesson. Despite winning ten NCAA national championships, Coach Wooden never focused on winning. He believed success was about doing everything to the best of your ability. Winning was simply the by-product of relentless effort.

He taught me that we cannot control results, but we can control our effort, our *focus*, and our attitude.

Leading with heart means showing up fully with passion, even when the outcome isn't guaranteed. It means pouring your heart into what you're doing and trusting the process.

So let me ask you:

- Are you leading with your heart, or are you caught up in chasing results?
- Do you approach life with the effort and passion that success demands, even when the outcome is uncertain?
- How are you showing up for yourself and others, regardless of the score?

Knowing your purpose is the path to true success. When you lead with your heart, you're on your way to success—even on the days you don't win. What matters isn't whether you hit the target; it's about the effort you put in and aiming with everything you've got.

The difference between mindset and purpose is the difference between seeing life and truly *living* it.

Looking back on my forty-year journey as a leader, I'm filled with gratitude. The girls I coached years ago, now grown women past their mid-twenties, still hug me when they see me. They remind me of something that touches my heart deeply: "Coach Bob, you were hard on us, but you cared."

That is what true leadership is about—tough but empathetic encouragement. It's not about being perfect but about discovering our strength, resilience, and potential and helping others do the same.

This philosophy extends beyond the soccer field or the workplace. It's the core of my mission: to inspire others to connect with their inner selves. Unlike motivation, which comes from external sources, inspiration is internal. It's the spark that comes from within and fuels meaningful, lasting change.

If there's one lesson I hope you take from my story, it's this: Believe in yourself from deep down in your heart, and know you can accomplish anything in life! Face every challenge head-on, and know that you will find the way. Stay focused on your purpose, know your *why*, and let that guide you through life.

The freedom I craved as a child has now become the pillar of my life to live by. I value the freedom to chart my own course, adhere to my own beliefs, and define success on my terms.

True success is not about going from point A to point B; rather, it's *the experience* of this journey called life!

The path to success is never a straight line. It's full of twists, turns, and lessons designed to shape you. Embrace the process, and trust in your ability to overcome.

When you focus on the journey, you'll find that success isn't the target you hit but *a way of life* and the leader you become along the way!

### ENDNOTES

1. "John Wooden Quotes," Quotefancy, accessed April 16, 2025, https://quotefancy.com/quote/845073/John-Wooden-Be-true-to-yourself-Be-true-to-those-you-lead.

2. "Henry Ford Quotes," accessed April 16, 2025, Goodreads, https://www.goodreads.com/quotes/978-whether-you-think-you-can-or-you-think-you-can-t--you-re.

## About Bob

Bob T. Kawabe, CFP, ChFC, CLU, CEPA, is the founder and principal of Kawabe Advisory Group, a firm dedicated to helping self-made, family-oriented business owners and entrepreneurs live their "Amazing Life of Significance." This is when they can spend time with those they care about and love, doing what they are passionate about and making an impact in the lives of others.

Bob has a deep passion for making a difference in the lives of others and helping them see their full potential. His mission has always been very clear: "To touch the lives of others to give hope so they can see all the possibilities, help them to define their true purpose in life, and inspire them to go after their dreams, as anything in life is possible."

Empowering others to believe in themselves and to dream as big as they want has always been at the core of what Bob stands for. Hearing all the "Noes" and "You cannots" as he was growing up has shaped Bob to become who he is today. Rather than believing in what he heard and letting those words limit him, he instead chose to believe in himself and to know that he could accomplish anything he wanted in life, and it was up to him to make it happen.

His own personal journey of seeing what was possible has fueled his mission to inspire others to do the same and to achieve their greatness. Bob inspires people to take action knowing they can achieve anything they want in life when they believe in themselves.

Life has always been about choices for Bob. As Henry Ford said, "Whether you think you can, or you think you can't—you're right."[2]

For this reason Bob has always chosen to believe that he *can*! He believes by choosing to shift our mindset on how we see things, and believing that we can, we begin to transform our realities. As everything starts in our minds, by changing our perspective on how we see things, it will begin to allow us to see all the new possibilities. For Bob, being able to help others shift their mindset from "No, I cannot," to "Yes, I can," has been the most rewarding part of what he does.

Bob's family has always been his solid foundation and inspiration. Growing up without a family to call his own, Bob truly understands and appreciates what it is like to have a true family. His wife, Janet, and their two children, Eden and Luke, are his greatest gifts and blessings. Janet is not only a loving wife and a mother to their children, but also his best friend. In his free time, Bob loves to surf, work out, read self-improvement books, and spend time having fun with his family.

You can learn more at Kawabeadvisorygroup.com.

# CHAPTER 7

# DIVINE GUIDANCE EMPOWERS PIVOTAL LEADERSHIP TRUTHS

By Linda Christensen

**D**eep within the earth, carbon undergoes transformation. An unremarkable element—dark, dull, overlooked—emerges as something extraordinary. It is not formed in comfort or shaped in ease. It is formed in depths where time, pressure, and heat turn it into something exceptional: diamonds. Each diamond's elegance comes from its multifaceted capacity to refract light.

Truth and leadership are forged in much the same way.

Imagine stepping into a dark room, unnerved by the thick blackness and what it may hide. But then—click—light illuminates everything, quieting your fears and revealing truths. Truths can drive change. These truths are not passive; they call us to action. They propel us toward new behaviors, replacing the seemingly impossible with a "mission possible" mindset. They ignite within us the courage to lead, love, and step into the highest version of who we are meant to be. And at the heart of it all, holding every facet together, is God—the Master Craftsman, who takes what is raw and unrefined and shapes it into something priceless. In His hands, our lives, our leadership, and our relationships become like diamonds—resilient, radiant, and undeniably valuable.

What if you are standing in the presence of *your* diamonds of truth, waiting to have your path and steps ahead illuminated?

Step forward. Pick them up. Let them change you. As I had to.

## LEADERSHIP BEGINS WITH SURRENDER

Leadership is often thought of as control—setting the course, steering the ship, making the decisions that shape outcomes. But the deeper truth, the hidden diamond, is that the most powerful leadership begins with surrender. It is found not in forcing our way forward but in trusting the One who desires to guide, direct, and carry us throughout our lives.

I learned this lesson not in a boardroom but in the unfolding reality of my own life.

For years I believed I was on a steady path. My career had been built with diligence, fueled by the discipline to achieve. I had my dream job. Then I met my future husband. We met at our workplace, both divorced after previous marriages. I had no children, and he had two young adult children, Dagny and Eric, and a fourteen-year-old daughter, Kira. Within the next year the need to pivot was both difficult and clear.

Two years later we enrolled at the University of South Carolina. The faculty adviser for accounting doctoral students was the landlord at our rental house! Was that God's providence again? Apparently yes! My assigned mentor expressed doubts regarding my doctoral candidacy, business experiences, and desire to teach rather than do research. Another needed pivot: I switched majors twice in the first year, finally settling on accounting, inspired by discussions with our landlord's husband.

Then, years later, my bid to become the dean of the college where my husband and I earned tenure appeared to be my next logical leadership role. It seemed like the culmination of all my efforts, the moment where preparation met purpose. And yet it didn't happen.

Failure has a way of refining us, much as pressure refines carbon into a diamond. My defining leadership moment was accepting that my greatest calling was not in leading an institution at all—it was in leading my family with unwavering love, courage, and faith. The decision to prioritize my husband, my children, and the integrity of our home over professional ambition became the most critical and defining act of leadership in my life.

That revelation didn't come easily. Life's unexpected turns tested us at every point. Looking back, I see God's hand orchestrating moments I could never have designed myself.

When I transitioned from accounting into international business, the opportunities that followed were beyond what I had ever envisioned. My life became a whirlwind of new experiences, traveling to France, Germany, Canada, Belgium, England, Mexico, and Venezuela. What once seemed impossible—an international career—became my reality. And yet just as quickly the demands of that world revealed their high cost. The excitement of the journey clashed with the truth that my heart longed for something more stable and connected to relationships at home.

Then came the next leap of faith: transitioning to academia.

When my husband and I decided to pursue PhDs at the University of South Carolina, we stepped into the unknown. We launched ourselves into rigorous study, intense pressure, and the challenges of balancing marriage, faith, and an uncertain future. And then, just as our doctoral study reached its peak, another layer of transformation unfolded. Before completing our degrees, our son Brett was born. I completed my dissertation while navigating the early days of motherhood, my new accounting faculty position, our new home, and my husband's new role on the finance faculty with his completed PhD. Our financial resources were stretched thin, our time even thinner, but God kept dropping breadcrumbs in our midst.

A cousin was unexpectedly assigned as my graduate assistant for that first year. Intense days of teaching, researching, and publishing filled the next years. So many challenges threatened to overwhelm us. Our daughter Tiffany was born in June at the end of our fourth year as tenure-track faculty. We accepted opportunities to teach in Slovakia during the summer one year after her birth. That five-week trip presented challenges and made us better teachers. A Christian colleague and his wife cared for our children while we traveled and taught. I felt assured and confident that our children would be loved, sheltered, and protected during our absence. Our daughter was so colicky before her first birthday that I got my first full night of sleep on that trip. How thankful I was for God's guidance and our friends' willingness to care for our children. Two years later we taught businesspeople in Slovakia when other Christian friends cared for our children. We were blessed to have friends who cared for our children when our calling took us across the world. How grateful we were for those experiences.

None of it was coincidence. All of it was God's leadership in action. Looking back, I see so many moments when I could have resisted, when I could have fought against the discomfort of change. I could have clung to my original plans, forcing a vision that was never meant to be. But true leadership isn't about forcing our own way forward. It's about trusting His way, even when it doesn't seem to make sense. God's leadership is not about making life easy. It is about making life meaningful. I didn't become a dean. But I became a mother, a wife, a mentor, and a teacher. I became the leader God intended me to be.

And in the end that is the only leadership that truly matters.

## The Leadership of Love

In life, as in leadership, we often default to what comes naturally. We follow the patterns we've learned, the methods that produce results, the paths of least resistance. The world teaches us that success comes from efficiency—find the quickest route, make the strongest move, and execute without hesitation. And while this approach might work in business, in academia, or even in personal achievement, it can quietly wreak havoc in relationships.

I saw it happening in my own home.

My husband was a star—highly respected at work, brilliant in his field, a man of discipline and unwavering consistency. His approach to life was regimented, clear-cut, and direct. He wasn't unkind, but to a sensitive person his words could land with a weight that felt heavier than intended.

Our children saw their dad's approach, and in their eyes it was the standard. His method got results. His authority ensured compliance. His discipline created order. But what about the unseen, unspoken parts of leadership, the parts that build relationships instead of just demanding results?

What about grace, empathy, timing, and connection? I wanted our children to see these. I wanted them to recognize and emulate how Jesus led—through patience, through discernment, through intention. His ways were so much more powerful and effective.

Sometimes when resistance is strong, force only strengthens it. And sometimes when people feel unheard, telling them what to do only makes them stop listening altogether.

This is where God's way of leadership differs from our natural instincts.

What comes naturally to us isn't always what's best for those around us. In our drive to get things done as quickly and effectively as possible, we can unintentionally bulldoze over emotions, fears, and unseen struggles. We can choose actions that dominate or coerce, manipulating situations to achieve the outcomes we want and prioritizing speed over empathy.

The world rewards results, but Jesus modeled *relationships*. When Jesus encountered resistance, He didn't respond with brute force. He knew that a heart softened by love will move more willingly than a heart hardened by pressure. What if instead of reacting out of frustration, we take time to understand what's beneath the surface? What if before issuing a command, we address the fears and discouragement that might cause resistance? What if rather than assuming obedience should be immediate, we make space for hearts and minds to willingly align with what's right?

When we take the time to recognize and confront emotions instead of dismissing them as obstacles, we set the stage for true, lasting cooperation.

Leadership isn't about who gets their way—it's about who is willing to do the *heart work* to bring people together.

I wanted our children to see that love is powerful, that listening is an important part of leading, and that grace builds what force can never sustain.

And in the moments where these ideas and my ways felt invisible, I had to remind myself that Jesus often worked in ways that the world didn't validate. And when we choose His way, we lead in a way that lasts.

## FROM THIRTY-FIVE THOUSAND FEET TO GROUND LEVEL

At thirty-five thousand feet, the world looks peaceful. The landscape is tranquil and quiet, the rivers that rage from the ground thread serenely through the valleys. From that vantage point everything seems calm and perfect. But life isn't lived at thirty-five thousand feet.

Life happens at ground level. It's in the words spoken at the dinner table, the heated exchanges in moments of stress, the decisions made in frustration or love. It's in the split-second choices we make during conflict, where our natural reactions—our defenses, our emotions—feel justified.

Most relationship advice stays at thirty-five thousand feet—offering general principles such as *be patient, be kind, forgive more,* and *love more.* And while those attitudes are crucial, they remain distant unless we bring them down to earth, into the dynamics of our *daily* conversations and conflicts.

Real transformation happens at ground level—where behaviors shift, responses change. It starts when we stop excusing our instincts and start intentionally reshaping them. When emotions run high, our default reactions feel natural. We raise our voices, shut down, deflect, attack, or withdraw—all in the name of self-preservation. We don't think of these as harmful; we think of them as *necessary—until* we see the damage they cause.

We can recognize how these defense mechanisms erode trust

and make real love and acceptance impossible. Proverbs 14:29 (NIV) says, "Whoever is patient has great understanding, but one who is quick-tempered displays folly." How often do we rush to defend ourselves without seeing the devastation left behind? The good news is that every destructive reaction has the potential to be transformed into something life-giving. Instead of reacting from instinct, we can respond with intention.

When someone is discouraged, instead of saying, "You need to try harder," say, "I see how hard you're trying. Let's figure out how to make this work." When someone is defensive, instead of saying, "That's not what I meant," say, "I understand why that upset you. Let's work through it together." Or when someone resists, soften your approach. Instead of saying, "You need to listen to me," say, "I want us to figure this out together."

When we desire to change, we stop seeing conflict as something to win. We start seeing it as something to heal. Jesus often modeled ground-level leadership. He demonstrated ground-level love. He knelt to wash feet, met people in their pain, responded with grace where others would have given judgment. And He calls us to do the same. The real work happens on the ground, in the smallest choices, in the everyday conversations where we get to decide, "Will I react out of frustration or respond with wisdom? Will I try to win or seek to understand? Will I demand my way or trust God's timing?"

When we choose ground-level transformation, relationships stop being battlegrounds—and become places of growth, healing, and love.

## THE GIFT OF GRACE

At the heart of every challenge, every relationship, and every unexpected turn in life, there lies a simple but profound truth: God is always leading us. The diamonds of truth that illuminate our paths are not rewards we must earn or treasures we must mine through our own efforts. They are gifts of grace, freely given, waiting to be discovered—not through striving but through surrender.

The greatest transformation in leadership, in love, and in life does not come from sheer willpower or perfect strategy. It comes from acknowledging God first, trusting His direction, and allowing His presence to refine us—just as pressure and heat refine carbon into diamond.

We do not need to prove ourselves worthy of His guidance. We do not need to fight to earn His acceptance. We are already fully loved, fully seen, and fully held in His hands. The moment we accept Christ as Lord and Savior, we are given a truth more valuable than any earthly treasure: We belong to Him. And because of that we can lead from a place of faith, not fear.

Overcoming discouragement is not about fighting harder— it's about trusting deeper. It's about surrendering our misguided desire to control and embracing His wisdom. His timing, His process, and His purpose are always greater than our own.

Some truths I pray you take with you are these: You don't have to do anything to earn God's love. You don't have to fight for His approval. You are already held, already cherished, already enough. God loves you when you wound His heart, when you walk away from Him, when you choose sin, when you resist saying, "I'm wrong," when you are wrapped in His arms of forgiveness, when you are welcomed back home. So embrace God's love. Be cleansed; be His child; rejoice in your homecoming. Let your heart reflect His love; do what others think is impossible. Step into what is already promised. Let His Holy Spirit inspire your leadership.

It's in faith that you'll find His leadership and presence in your heart and mind. Believe in His diamonds of grace and love. Let His diamonds of truth permeate your heart and be reflected in your life.

## About Linda

Linda Christensen has achieved success in business and leadership over the past fifty years. She is passionate about God and His love and desire to guide and influence our lives and our leadership. Since retiring from academia, she coauthored two books, *Mission ImPossible* and *Diamonds of Truth*. She is passionate about the content of her books and their relevance for today's business leaders. During more than twenty-two years at universities, her classes contributed to preparing many undergraduate and graduate students for leadership roles in business. Before she retired from academia, she taught classes about ethics in accounting where real-world cases demonstrated how much our world cries out for more honest and ethical leaders.

Linda completed her BSBA at the University of Missouri, Certified Public Accountant licensure in Tennessee, MBA at the University of Memphis, and PhD in business administration at the University of South Carolina. She taught at Wichita State University, Union University, and Christian Brothers University.

God gave Linda and Donald Christensen the gift of marriage in 1983. For almost thirty-two years they shared their love and the love of their children, Dagny, Eric, Kira, Brett, and Tiffany, and grandchildren, Jerry, Danielle, Ethan, Andrew, Christian, and Wyatt.

Linda is the oldest of seven siblings who each made public confessions of faith in God as young teenagers. The love of their mother and father and the Bible's examples encouraged Linda. Her immediate family and grandparents, aunts, uncles, cousins, and friends afforded many opportunities to experience and observe personalities and successful relationships. Linda is passionate about family relationships, Christian books, and Bible studies. She values and rejoices over God's gifts provided by the Christian counselors, leaders, and friends who modeled and shared true Christian love. She believes He inspired and guided the stories and observations incorporated within her books as well as her leadership experiences throughout her life.

Linda enjoys being creative, designing, and especially traveling and spending time with family and friends. Also, her newest grandchild, Emily, brings great joy and love to Linda's life.

# CHAPTER 8

# THE LEADERSHIP EVOLUTION

*From Control to Collaboration*

---

By Cain Daniel

The ceiling was low, and the air was musty, but the moisture in the walls could not dampen our determination. The hum of a space heater did its best to ward off the chill, and a single light bulb flickered above. Joe's desk—if you could call it that—was barely holding together, one leg propped up with a stack of old textbooks. I didn't even have a desk, just a laptop I balanced on my legs. I had joined my friend Joe White on the business he had started, REMIC, the Real Estate and Mortgage Institute of Canada. We had high hopes and believed in what we were building, so at first, the hustle was exhilarating.

We were in the trenches, bootstrapping everything, fueled by a start-up spirit and convinced that the success of our venture depended entirely on how hard we were willing to work. We were answering phones, designing our own web pages, running marketing, cold-calling leads, even scrubbing the bathroom when we finally upgraded to a real office.

But the more we grew, the more I felt as if I were drowning. I told myself no one could handle things like I could, so I made every decision and micromanaged every detail. And that's when the business that was supposed to set me free threatened to keep me in a prison of perfection!

# THE POWER OF LETTING GO

For a long time I thought leadership meant doing everything myself, that the success of our business rested entirely on my ability to control every detail. I am obsessed over things like the exact shade of blue in our logo, the spacing between words on a flyer, the phrasing of every email. I battled with designers, second-guessed every piece of marketing material, and spent hours fine-tuning things that didn't move the needle.

What I didn't realize at the time was that my perfectionism wasn't helping—it was *hurting*. Perfection is the enemy of progress. While I was busy making sure a logo was pixel-perfect, I wasn't making sales. While I was stressing over the layout of a webpage, I wasn't out in the field, building the relationships that would actually grow our business. I had convinced myself that if I wasn't involved in every detail, things would fall apart. But the truth? I was the one slowing us down.

Late nights turned into early mornings, and my stress skyrocketed. I wasn't managing my time and was drowning in my own refusal to let go. I didn't wake up one morning and magically decide to let go. It happened in phases. At first, delegation wasn't a choice—it was a necessity. I physically couldn't do it all anymore. We had to hire and trust people. As uncomfortable as it was, I could breathe again.

At first, I worried, "What if they didn't do things my exact way? What if something wasn't perfect?" What I learned is that most people are competent. The work got done. The company moved forward. It wasn't always exactly how I would have done it, but that was OK.

The truth is, leadership isn't about *doing*—it's about *guiding*. When I stopped trying to control everything and started trusting the people around me, not only did our business grow, but I grew. I became a better leader, a better strategist, and a better person. By assigning tasks based on each employee's strengths, leaders free up valuable time and cultivate a culture of trust and innovation.

In fact, studies have shown that leaders who delegate effectively enjoy an average revenue increase of 33 percent, highlighting how smart delegation not only boosts productivity but also significantly drives business growth. Letting go wasn't losing control—it was gaining freedom. And that freedom allowed me to focus on what really mattered: scaling REMIC, driving sales, and creating something that could thrive without me having my hands on every single detail.

If you want to grow personally and professionally, you have to learn to delegate. Trust the process. Trust your people. And most importantly, trust that progress, even if imperfect, is always better than perfection that never happens.

## The Power of Self-Awareness

One of the most eye-opening moments in my leadership journey came when someone told me, "You're not very approachable." At first, I was shocked. *Me? Not approachable?* I had always considered myself kind, easygoing—someone people could talk to. But when I sat with that feedback, I had to face a hard truth: Perception and reality aren't always the same thing.

I *felt* approachable. But when I really thought about it, I realized that people weren't coming to me with ideas. They weren't casually stopping by my office to chat. Why? Because I was so focused and serious about the work that my mannerisms, my expressions—maybe even my energy—sent a different message.

This realization hit me hard. If people didn't feel comfortable talking to me, that meant they weren't bringing me their best ideas. They weren't giving me honest feedback. They weren't sharing concerns before they became problems. That's a dangerous place for any leader to be.

I had unknowingly created a barrier, not because I was unkind but because I wasn't intentional about showing people that I *wanted* their input.

Self-awareness in leadership isn't about how *you feel*—it's about how *others experience* you.

I had to shift my radar. If I wanted my team to express themselves, I had to show them that I truly valued their voices.

I started to think about how *I* liked to be led. I wanted independence and freedom, but not everyone feels that way. Some people need reassurance, guidance, and collaboration. Leadership isn't one-size-fits-all. So I changed my approach. I started having one-on-one conversations with my team—not just about work but about how they liked to work. I was honest and accountable about my blind spots and made it clear that I *wanted* to hear from them. I focused on adapting my leadership style to each individual instead of assuming everyone was wired like me.

And the result? More creativity. More innovation. A stronger culture. The lesson here is simple: It's not enough to assume you're a good leader—you have to check the mirror. I've learned that one of the most crucial aspects of effective leadership is self-awareness, especially when it comes to avoiding a power differential between me and my team. In the past I created unintended barriers by isolating myself or unintentionally projecting the message that I was the "untouchable" leader. It wasn't out of ego; it was just a lack of awareness.

If you're in any position of leadership, at work, at home, in your community, I encourage you to find out what messages you're sending. How do people experience you? Are they comfortable bringing you new ideas? Do they feel seen and heard? Self-awareness is a game-changer. When you learn to see yourself as others do—and make adjustments—you unlock the full potential of the people around you. And that's when real leadership begins.

## THE POWER OF INCLUSION

For a long time Joe and I did all the hiring. We handled everything—posting the job, screening résumés, conducting interviews, making final decisions. We didn't ask for input from the people who would actually be working with these new hires. We thought we were being efficient. In reality, we were missing a huge opportunity.

Then, something shifted. As we embraced a mindset of collaboration, we started questioning our approach. Why weren't we including our team in these decisions? After all, they were the ones who would work with these people day in and day out. Their input wasn't just valuable—it was *essential*.

We reimagined our hiring process. Instead of just relying on résumés and traditional interviews, we introduced video submissions. Candidates sent in a short video about *why* they wanted to work with us and invited our team to watch and weigh in.

In the first round I would screen the videos and short-list candidates. For the second round our team members met with the candidates. These were informal conversations—an opportunity for candidates to ask real questions, the kind they might not feel comfortable asking a founder or manager. Then, the entire team weighed in on the final decision, and everyone had to agree. Each hire was a *true* team hire.

Our staff felt more ownership, more investment in the people we brought in, and it improved our company culture. When you involve others, you create alignment, engagement, and stronger outcomes.

Had we continued hiring the way we always had, we would've kept building a business *for* our employees instead of *with* them. The takeaway? Be flexible. Be open. Trust your team. Because when everyone has a voice, you create an environment in which everyone is moving together toward a shared purpose.

Looking back, I can see just how much I had to unlearn in order to grow—not just as a business owner but as a leader. I started out believing that success meant doing everything myself, controlling every detail, and pushing harder when things got tough. But that approach nearly broke me.

It wasn't until I embraced trust, self-awareness, and inclusion that I realized what leadership is really about. Delegation didn't make me weaker—it made our business stronger. Self-awareness didn't just help me connect with my team; it helped me unlock their full potential. And when I stopped making decisions in a vacuum and started bringing my people into the process? We didn't just build a business. We built a culture. As John C. Maxwell wisely put it, "A leader is one who knows the way, goes the way, and shows the way."[1]

I learned that to be truly successful, I couldn't just be the leader. True success came when I learned to empower *others* to be leaders themselves.

### ENDNOTE

1.    "30 Best John C. Maxwell Quotes With Image," Bookey.com, accessed April 16, 2025, https://www.bookey.app/quote-author/john-c.-maxwell.

## About Cain

With over a decade of leadership in professional education, Cain Daniel has helped thousands of entrepreneurs break into and excel in the financial services industry. As a business leader, he has demonstrated success in sales, marketing, operations, and the development of innovative strategies.

Cain is a partner at REMIC and serves as vice president. REMIC is a leading educational institute for financial services throughout Canada. He has also cofounded AMIPROS, an association dedicated to educating mortgage professionals and the public about investing in mortgages.

Cain is driven by his mission to transform students into successful entrepreneurs. His passion for innovative training has equipped individuals with the essential tools and strategies necessary to achieve success in their entrepreneurial journeys. Most recently, Cain colaunched the *Billionaire Dollar Podcast*, where he and industry leaders share insights and stories to inspire entrepreneurs to make their mark in any industry.

Outside the office, Cain channels his competitive spirit into playing soccer and also enjoys his downtime with his wife and their two children, Mila and Evan.

You can learn more at caindaniel.com or remic.ca.

CHAPTER 9

# THE DEFINITION OF *LEADERSHIP* IS NOT PERFECTION

By Dr. Veronica Whittington

I n 2006 a man named John Koenig began a construction project. His goal?

To fill the voids left by the English language, to give sound and structure to those vague emotions we all feel but struggle to describe.

He called his project *The Dictionary of Obscure Sorrows*, and perhaps the most well-known word to come out of it is "sonder."

*Sonder* is "the realization that every stranger around you lives a vivid, complex life—filled with their own ambitions, struggles, and unseen madness—an epic story that continues around you like an anthill sprawling deep underground, with elaborate passageways to thousands of other lives that you'll never know existed, in which you might appear only once, as an extra sipping coffee in the background, as a blur of traffic passing on the highway, as a lighted window at dusk."

Fascinating concept, isn't it? Sonder reminds us that everyone carries hidden struggles, much like the doubts and fears that often shape leaders. Recognizing this shared humanity is the first step to leading with empathy.

Things like the hopelessness of poverty, the devastation of heartbreak, and the humiliation of failure, the self-consciousness that comes with being "wrong." The wrong answer, the wrong person, the wrong idea, the fear of one's imperfections being on display for all to see.

The fear of being found out.

Inner stories are a calamity no one is immune to. The voices of negative programming are equal-opportunity enemies, plaguing each of us at one time or another.

From wherever you're reading this, someone nearby is running a company, is falling in love, or just accomplished a long-held goal.

And there's a good chance that every one of their psyches is punctured with doubt.

I can relate to this.

I've always worked methodically from one goal to the next, steadily marching forward to chart my own path. In high school I got special permission to take additional classes, allowing me to get a head start on my journey toward a career in the medical field. I completed college-level courses during my junior and senior years of high school and graduated as president of my nursing class. I attended medical school and matched into a general-surgery residency. I had a similar education and the same drive and in many cases had overcome challenges my peers couldn't even fathom, yet I had accumulated enough shame around my shortcomings that I became a prisoner of my own self-criticism.

You've probably heard of the term *impostor syndrome*, but what I've learned over the years is that thinking we have impostor syndrome is incomplete at best. What happens when you *are* the high achiever and you *do* believe you belong among the great, but you're ashamed of your imperfections?

I want to challenge the idea of impostor syndrome. Most successful people don't truly doubt themselves—if they did, they wouldn't try, let alone succeed. The real issue isn't doubt; it's *shame*. We don't doubt our abilities; we're ashamed of our imperfections. It begins when we prioritize others' values over our own—like pursuing a "respectable" career to please your family instead of following your passions. On a deeper level you're rejecting yourself. Over time this rejection of self convinces you that your values are wrong or invalid. That's pretty painful. For me shame meant rejecting the totality of who I was. It was OK for others to have flaws, but I couldn't give myself the same grace.

Perhaps you've been there.

You know your worth, but the voice of shame pulls you right back. This vicious cycle continues because the root cause is unrealized. Like a tire with a hidden puncture, shame keeps us deflated until we address the root cause.

Shame is triggered when we fall short of our *own* standards. These standards form in childhood and are shaped by families and societies we grow up in. If you belonged to a family that valued academic excellence, receiving criticism or rejection for a D or F would cause you to reject the part of you that didn't value the academic pursuit enough to want to score high grades. This happens because our primal need for love, safety, and belonging is threatened when we don't meet imposed expectations. To break this cycle, I designed a framework that reflects on your choices and uncovers what truly resonates with *you*.

Shame thrives when we believe we fall short. These feelings whisper that we're missing something essential. But to move beyond shame, we must come to know and accept ourselves fully. True leadership begins with this self-awareness. What if those cracks are the spaces our light gets to shine through? What if the things we think are lacking are what set us apart as extraordinary?

Throughout my journey I've learned that I cannot find peace in my life while engaged in war against myself.

I would need to learn to quiet the voice of self-doubt and accept the totality of who I was, not as a bundle of imperfections but a kaleidoscope of experiences.

You can do this too by leaning in to the very things you've been rejecting about yourself.

When you're feeling the pain of not belonging, consider this: Belonging is our natural state, while fitting in demands we shapeshift to meet others' expectations. So if belongings refer to possessions, then your belonging is something you're in possession of.

What better thing to be in possession of than the essence of yourself?

## LEADERS KNOW THEMSELVES

"Get to the hospital, now," my mother said, her voice anxious with concern. I was nine months pregnant and had been laboring all night.

I've always been a strong, healthy person. I'd found out I was pregnant after just starting my surgical residency and wanted to have a natural water birth. Although the pregnancy wasn't planned, I still thought I had control and could map out a natural delivery, as I'd mapped out every other endeavor of my career.

My body had other ideas.

As soon as I got to the hospital, everything unraveled. The first failure was a missed IV, and shortly after that the baby's heart began to race, barring me from the water birth I'd envisioned. The epidural was the next betrayal, a needle stabbing into the wrong place, blood pooling where it shouldn't have. Hours crawled by in a haze of exhaustion, until the grim announcement came: The baby's heart was racing too fast for too long. A C-section was inevitable. I was consumed by anger. My baby's heart had been racing since I had arrived at the hospital twelve hours before, and it was only now that they considered it an emergency!

My husband was unsupportive, dismissing my anguish, and it wasn't long before I felt that my body, my marriage, and the medical system I'd spent my life serving were all conspiring against me. And yet in the eye of this storm, my daughter arrived perfect and healthy. A week later I left my husband and my residency, and in the quiet aftermath, with titles of wife and surgeon stripped away, I met someone I'd lost long ago—myself.

You see, there's a layer to knowing yourself that you don't experience until you're stripped of all the labels. It's destabilizing, uncomfortable, and vital to your growth.

Once we know who we are, we can begin to align our actions

with our values. This alignment is the foundation for inspired leadership—bridging the gap between who we are and who we aspire to be.

We know what kind of ice cream we like but are unfamiliar with the furthest stretches of our boundaries.

We know where we like to shop but get lost in the depths of our own values, reverting to ones imposed on us from childhood.

We know what clothes we like to wear but lose our way when called upon to act from the deepest recesses of our hearts.

That level of awareness *can* come by choice, but for most of us it comes unexpectedly, summoning us to a moment of reckoning during which we can retreat into ignorance or rise to meet the highest version of ourselves.

I chose to rise. And you can too.

Every unexpected pivot, whether it's as small as a disrupted schedule or as shocking as a disrupted life, is an invitation to lead.

Can you describe yourself without using any of your labels or titles? What moves you? What passions keep your inner fire lit? What do you stand for and against?

When you can answer those questions and use them as a decision-making guide from which you do not deviate, your inner leader is awake.

## LEADERS MIND THE GAP

The light on my beeper flashed, summoning me to the room of a new patient I hadn't yet seen. I was in my surgical residency at the time, and while I was prepared for any kind of medical emergency, I was not prepared for a lesson in morality.

The patient was a prisoner, shackled to the bed, his bloody face and broken jaw a grotesque result of a prison brawl. Blood stained the sheets, and though his appearance was menacing, there was a fragility in him that pierced through my clinical detachment. In that moment, I didn't see a violent inmate but a vulnerable patient. I didn't know his crime, only his pain, and it was my duty to help him. When I ordered pain medication, the nurse hesitated. "Give it to him now," I commanded, grounding myself in the principle that leadership is not about judgment—it's about action rooted in integrity. An hour later I returned to find him calmer, and he expressed his gratitude for my help. That moment crystallized a truth: Leadership demands that we rise above our biases to see humanity in others. To lead is to remain anchored in your values, never allowing external details to dilute your character. In every role of authority, from surgeon to leader, the power to alleviate suffering carries a responsibility—to act with compassion, without judgment.

According to Brené Brown, the space between our practiced values (what we do) and our aspirational values (what we wish we were doing) is our values gap.

One of the principles of inspired leadership that has served me well is to follow my values even when they are unpopular.

As you reflect on your own experiences, think about moments you were called to lead—not by title or position but by circumstances that demanded action. Were you able to mind the gap between your practiced and aspirational values? Did you rise to meet the challenge with compassion even when it felt uncomfortable or unpopular?

Leadership, after all, is not about perfection—it's about progress, and progress demands action. Sometimes lives—our own or others'—depend on it. It's about the willingness to confront those moments of moral tension and choose a path that aligns with your highest principles. So the next time you're called to lead, will you step into the gap? And when you do, what will your actions say about the values you hold most dear?

## A Leader Acts Fast

"He's not moving air," I shouted in a tone that pressed for a swift response.

The patient was clearly in distress. I was a nurse at the time, and though I called for backup, it was slow to come. There was no time to doubt myself or grapple with the fact that technically I didn't have the authority to save this patient. If I stopped to question my own ability, this man was going to die. I began directing staff, grabbed an aid from the hallway to help me move him into the bed, initiated the code, and began chest compressions.

After just a few minutes that seemed like hours, I heard the timid beep of his heart beating again.

As the adrenaline subsided, I thought about what had happened. All the regret from moments I'd hesitated melted away, and reality sunk in. This patient was alive because I took the lead.

The leader within us often lies dormant until the moment demands we rise. When the stakes are high, something awakens. In those moments, our self-imposed limitations crumble, irrelevant in the face of our mission to serve, protect, and uplift. Adversity becomes the spark that ignites the leader in us, a reminder that our power is born from the courage to meet the impossible head-on, for the sake of something greater than ourselves.

In any decision you make, ask yourself, "If a life depended on this, what would I do?" And then do it. Because a life *does* depend on it—*yours*.

## LEADERS LOVE THEMSELVES

Years ago in nursing school I did a pediatric rotation. One of my patients was a little boy suffering from a congenital defect that left him with impaired hearing and speech. He loved video games, and during my breaks, instead of hanging in the nurse's lounge, I made my way to Timmy's room for our daily video game competitions.

A few weeks later, as I was walking to my car, I heard someone call my name. It was Timmy. He had been released from the hospital, and his little body was running toward me at full speed. He jumped into my arms, and my heart exploded with gratitude.

This is what it's about.

Being present. Honoring our values. Leading with heart.

Life will change, seasons will change, years will pass, but the one constant is us. We start and end each day with ourselves.

Embracing the totality of who we are is the most courageous act of leadership we can demonstrate. To see our differences not as burdens but as gifts, not as flaws but as the seeds of genius and connection, is to step into a power that cannot be shaken. True leadership is born in the quiet revolution of self-acceptance—when we stop asking, "What am I missing?" and start proclaiming, "This is who I am."

I know this because I've lived it. I was a child, dreaming of a life I couldn't yet name. Today, I stand as a medical professional, a mother, a coach, a mentor, and now an author, a speaker, and an entrepreneur! My journey hasn't been perfect, but it's been mine. And in embracing every piece of it—every struggle, every triumph—I found my essence, the leader.

I hope in reading this you are inspired to embark on your own journey—to live an empowered life, pursue meaningful goals, and nurture your family in a way that no one else can duplicate. When you discover your truth, the leader within you will enrich your contributions to society and to those closest to you, with what they need most: the essence of you.

*As you step into your authentic leadership—the irreplaceable you—the world will be forever changed in ways only you can achieve.*

## About Veronica

Dr. Veronica Whittington is a transformational leader, mentor, and visionary, redefining what it means to live, lead, and create global impact. With a multidisciplinary background in medicine, hypnosis, and negotiation, Veronica empowers the world's most affluent and high-performing individuals to achieve personal transformation while spearheading initiatives that create profound humanitarian change.

As the founder of the Human Experience Framework (HEF), Veronica created this groundbreaking system as the antidote to achieving her ultimate vision: Redefining the Human Experience™. This mission is a call to action to shift how the world approaches human existence, making what's wrong in the world right again. By addressing global challenges such as clean-water access, sustainable energy, human safety, and the infrastructure that connects the globe, Veronica envisions a future where esteemed leaders around the world experience profound personal transformation while achieving unprecedented, meaningful, and lasting change.

Veronica's journey began with her own struggles, navigating the demands of success and leadership while seeking deeper fulfillment. She understands firsthand the weight of high-stakes decision-making and the isolation that often accompanies it. She revels in creating a safe haven of vulnerability and confidentiality—an invaluable space rarely found at the highest levels of success. For those accustomed to carrying the burdens of leadership alone, this sanctuary offers the freedom to reflect, realign, and reconnect with their deeper purpose. Inspired to bridge the gap between achievement and fulfillment, she developed HEF to unlock limitless potential, align personal truth with action, and redefine leadership on a global scale.

Through her work Veronica has helped visionary leaders break free from societal expectations, reconnect with their core values, and channel their success into transformative global initiatives. Her programs inspire freedom, fulfillment, and purpose, equipping leaders to make their mark on history while building a better world.

At the heart of her mission lies a belief in the power of aligned leadership to create a ripple effect of transformation—one leader at a time.

In her upcoming work, an autobiography hybrid, *Redefining the*

*Human Experience™: Finding Truth, Power, and Transformation*, she delves into experiences and insights that inspired the creation of Redefining the Human Experience™ and challenges her readers to unlearn some of society's most debilitating paradigms.

Learn more about Veronica's revolutionizing work at www.HEFramework. com, or email Info@heframework.com to begin your journey toward unparalleled transformation and impact.

# CHAPTER 10

# THE BEST IS YET TO COME

By Kellye Alsop

T he rain hammered against the window, echoing the tears streaming down my face. Lightning cracked through the sky, illuminating the bedroom for a moment before plunging it back into darkness.

The feeling of isolation was heavy. My sisters had moved out, and my stepmother—the one person who made me feel taken care of—was gone. At sixteen years old, I had emptied my savings to help her escape my father's abuse, but now I was left behind to deal with his alcoholism and gambling. I remember vowing to myself that I would never be dependent on a man, and never be trapped in a soul-crushing situation because of a lack of resources. For a moment, the storm raging outside was nothing compared with the storm within me. My best friend's mother had just died of cancer, and I remember thinking she was the lucky one, that perhaps I'd be better off if I were no longer here.

The ache in my chest was unbearable, but I was still aware enough to know that my thoughts had entered a dark place, and I needed help. I picked up the phone and called my friend. "Drive over here," he said. I don't remember much about the drive, only that I ended up staying there, finding a sliver of solace in the presence of someone who cared.

That night wouldn't be the last time my thoughts landed me in a dark place. The pain of abandonment, the regret of sacrifices, and the relentless challenges that came with trying to hold a family together would follow me throughout my adult life.

Ten years after that night in my bedroom, I married my boss, a wealthy doctor, had seven children with him, and quickly forgot the vow I had made to myself, leaving behind a lucrative career in finance to raise the kids. We had a beautiful home, but when the real-estate market crashed in 2008, our marriage fell apart. I was left homeless with the youngest two of my seven kids and was completely devastated! I had given him the best years of my life, and now I was alone—again.

Divorce is a death that no one mourns with you. It's a tearing apart that feels as if your very soul is being ripped in half. I had sacrificed my career in finance, one I loved and excelled at, to raise our seven children and build the happy family I had always dreamed of. When the marriage fell apart, it was like watching a lifetime of dreams shatter into pieces I could never put back together. I was past childbearing years, past the years one grows a career, and thought, "This is it—there will never be another chance for the family I always longed for."

I felt too old to start over, too old to go back to my career, too old for pretty much anything. I don't remember the exact moment, but at some point, my sadness transformed into a fierce determination, and I knew that it was not too late for anything.

I made up my mind that every challenge, every betrayal, every abandonment was a gift in disguise. I decided that if I could reawaken the wisdom I had stored over the years from the books I had read and the experiences I had lived through, there was always a lesson to learn, always a chance to start over, and always a reason to believe that the best is yet to come.

## REJECTION IS PROTECTION

Rejection was an early theme in my life. When I was two weeks old, my mother abandoned me. My sister and I were sent to live with my grandparents in the country away from my siblings. For the longest time, I resented that. I felt that there must have been something wrong with me to be discarded like unwanted garbage.

As I grew older, I read about how we must trust that anything

THE BEST IS YET TO COME

that happens, happens *for* us, not *to* us. That plane you missed may have been the one that crashed. That traffic may have saved you from a car accident. It occurred to me then that the kids who had stayed in my parents' home all ended up with dysfunctional lives and addiction issues. I, on the other hand, had grown up with loving grandparents who made me cookies, encouraged my creativity, and taught me how to genuinely connect with people.

Rejection, change, and inconvenience are all forms of protection. Now, even the dissolution of my marriage feels like a gift that liberated me from a relationship in which I was never valued.

We are never being rejected. We are being fortified, prepared, and awakened to our true strength. Take every unexpected change not as a loss but a redirection toward what's meant for you.

## Joy Is a Choice

I grew up surrounded by challenges. My parents were alcoholics, and my siblings smoked. It would have been easy to follow the path laid before me, but I made a choice to rise above my circumstances. I turned to education and devoured books such as *Chicken Soup for the Soul*, stories of people who inspired me with their resilience and strength. I watched movies about overcoming adversity and learned that no matter where you are, you can rise. This realization became my foundation, the truth that shaped my destiny.

When my husband left me and our youngest two children homeless, it was one of the darkest times of my life. By day we were homeless; by night we sought refuge in an office building. But even in those moments, I refused to be defeated. I started taking action. I launched several businesses: a cleaning service, a landscaping company, and a handyman service. At the height of the foreclosure crisis I found work cleaning up foreclosed homes. Every step was fueled by a belief that there was a way forward.

Happiness is a choice. During this challenging time someone gave me a Joyce Meyer CD series. We listened to it over and over until we practically knew it by heart. One morning when my heart felt particularly heavy, my little one sensed it and repeated a line from the CD: "We're just goin' to have a good time anyway!" That moment became a turning point. I chose to have a good time no matter what!

Trader Joe's became a fun outing with free samples. Blockbuster Video offered a free DVD each day that summer, and my children, who previously had only watched *Reading Rainbow*, now had access to entertainment. These little moments reminded me that joy is a deliberate choice.

Jack Canfield's principles resonated deeply with me, especially the idea of taking 100 percent responsibility for your life. He said something that stuck with me: "*You can always learn from everything, even if it's just learning what not to do.*" That perspective changed everything. I realized I didn't need to know the entire path ahead; I just needed to take the next step and trust that the rest would unfold.

My faith became a pillar of strength. Jeremiah 29:11 reminded me that there is a plan for each of us: "*'For I know the plans I have for you,' declares the Lord, 'plans to prosper you and not to harm you, plans to give you hope and a future'*" (NIV). Even when I felt unseen or unworthy, I held on to this promise. I went to church, found inspiration in fitness icon Jack LaLanne, and embraced the idea that wellness is a matter of not just personal but spiritual security. My work, no matter the employer, became my service to God. I wasn't just surviving—I was building a life of purpose.

Today, I continue to grow. I have read hundreds of books, have taught the principles of legendary trainer John Maxwell, and am in the process of completing a second HeartCore Leadership training. Each step in this journey has taught me that our circumstances don't define us—our choices do. Taking 100 percent responsibility isn't about blame or guilt; it's about power and ownership. It's the ultimate declaration that you are the author of your story.

Now I invite you to reflect:

- What circumstances in your life have you allowed to dictate your path?

- What would it look like to take full responsibility for where you are and where you're going?
- What's one small step you can take today to move closer to the life you want?

Remember, you don't need to have all the answers. Just take the next step. The path will reveal itself as you move forward. And as you walk, carry this truth with you: You are capable of rising above anything. Your destiny is yours to create.

## WHEN ALL ELSE FAILS, GIVE

One of the toughest parts about navigating a divorce is that often kids will be mad. The catalyst for the divorce is irrelevant. Kids have big feelings, they need to put those feelings somewhere, and often, fair or not, it will land on the mother!

Not long ago I was feeling the heartache of my children's disdain, and the dark, familiar thoughts crept in my mind.

"What's the point? Why should I even get out of bed today?"

A voice clear as day came into my mind and said, "Because of the sisters."

I remembered then that the best way to dilute pain is through service.

At the time, I was teaching a yoga class, and after each class, I would put out a spread of healthy food and invite my clients to stay and connect. Every week, the same two sisters attended my class. One of the sisters was born healthy but was partially paralyzed following complications in childhood. I found out that these two sisters, who lived two freeway exits from the yoga studio, were walking to my class every week. They loved the community so much that every week, the one pushed her sister's walker to class, and back again after dark. I was touched and dumbfounded that they would go to those lengths just to attend my class! That morning, I promised to give them a ride. It didn't take long for my thoughts to shift from despair to gratitude. The sisters needed me, I had the capacity to help, and I would get out of bed and get them to class!

I was pretty young when I read the book *How to Win Friends and Influence People*, and I learned that no matter what was happening to me, I could shift my energy by giving to someone else, whether it was through an act of service or a sincere compliment.

Since then, I have worked tirelessly with the Office of Disaster Recovery and Resilience, working with people whose lives have been shaken by catastrophe. I was sent to Hawaii after the wildfires and found myself speaking with and encouraging people who had lost their entire families and homes to the flames. Not long ago, when my dad became sick, I found myself completely responsible for the care of his seventh wife, who was suffering from Alzheimer's. She required round-the-clock attention, and it would have been easy to take a "not my problem" stance, but my beliefs wouldn't allow that. Instead, I committed to figuring out how I could make the biggest difference for her.

I put her on the stationary bike, changed her diet, and took her to church, and before long her health and her disposition completely changed, and she was able to read and write again. She even wrote me a thank-you note!

No matter how heavy the burden or how overwhelming the storm, your character remains your compass. The good you do, the lives you touch, and the lessons you carry with you are indelible marks on the world—things no one can ever take away. In those moments when it feels as if there's nothing left, remember, you are the sum of your resilience, your compassion, and your determination to rise no matter how many times you're knocked down.

## YOUR LOT IS YOUR GIFT

The pastor's words stayed with me: "You have a lot to deal with."

He knew I was taking care of my dad's wife, and at first, I heard his words as a testament to my burden, but the more I thought about it, the more I realized the truth of it—we *all* have a *lot*.

Our lot in life isn't a fixed sentence; it's a movable thing, shaped by what we choose to do with it. For years I resented the belief that I had given away the best years of my life. I told myself that if I had stayed in finance, I could have been a millionaire. But I've come to see the truth: I didn't give away the best years of my life—I spent them *becoming* the person I was meant to be. I learned from Jack Canfield, John Maxwell, Jack LaLanne, Stephen Covey, Wayne Dyer, and countless others that life is less about what happens to you and more about what you do with it. Now, with more than half my life ahead of me, I am determined to make the last half the *best* half.

And so I turn this back to you. What is *your* lot? What will you do with it? Remember, it's not set in stone. It can be shaped, shifted, and transformed. You haven't lost anything. Nothing has been wasted.

Life is meant to be lived in full-spectrum color, and we are meant to derive wisdom and growth from both the light and the dark. And to always trust, with unwavering faith, that the best is yet to come.

## About Kellye

Kellye Alsop is a dynamic transformational coach, author, speaker, fitness trainer, and instructor who is deeply committed to promoting a vibrant and healthy lifestyle. Despite facing a challenging childhood, including abandonment and significant trauma, Kellye transformed her mindset from victim to victor. She overcame obstacles such as suicidal thoughts, job loss, rape, divorce, and empty-nest syndrome, emerging stronger and more determined to live a life full of purpose and vitality.

By the age of twenty-five, Kellye had already built a diverse career, managing a health club, a vitamin store, and a financial institution. Later in life, as a mother of seven, she skillfully balanced the demands of a bustling household while also caring for her ninety-five-year-old grandfather. His peaceful passing, just shy of his one hundredth birthday, provided Kellye with lasting insights on how to live—and die—well. This experience deepened her commitment to holistic wellness, leading her to launch *Greatest Gainer*, a show dedicated to a healthy lifestyle and mindset. Her focus is not simply on weight loss but on empowering individuals to embrace long-term wellness in all aspects of life.

Throughout her career Kellye has helped countless individuals overcome health challenges such as high blood pressure, medication dependency, and mental health struggles. Many have even avoided heart surgery through her guidance. Recently, her work has expanded to support those affected by Alzheimer's and dementia, a growing concern in today's society. Her empowering mantra, "The Best Is Yet to Come," inspires others to build resilience, wellness, and freedom in every aspect of their lives.

Kellye's name, which has Irish roots meaning "warrior princess," is a fitting tribute to her indomitable spirit and dedication to helping others thrive. Her journey into holistic health began after a pivotal moment during a school field trip, when she realized the importance of teaching children the fundamentals of taking care of their bodies. This led her to explore alternative educational sources, eventually homeschooling her own children and later discovering The NEWSTART program, a health approach developed by the Seventh-day Adventists. This program, focused on nutrition, exercise, water, sunlight, temperance, air, rest, and trust in God, became central to Kellye's approach to health and wellness.

Throughout her career Kellye has worked with multiple health clubs, including Jack LaLanne European Health Clubs, and managed a vitamin store, where she learned the importance of supplementation. Her own experiences overcoming life's challenges have given her the grit and a blueprint for helping others navigate their own paths to wellness.

Kellye's book, *Don't Shoot Yourself, or Simply Thrive: How to Thrive Thru Divorce*, shares her personal story of overcoming pain and finding strength during life's toughest trials. As she looks to the future, Kellye is driven to assist as many people as possible in developing a healthy, balanced lifestyle—physically, mentally, and emotionally—so they too can heal, overcome, and thrive.

# CHAPTER 11

# LEADERSHIP IS BUILT IN THE WRECKAGE

By Rose Barr

The camera on the desk crackled to life, alerting me to the fact that there was activity on our doorstep.

We had just moved to Santa Fe, New Mexico, for what was supposed to be an exciting new chapter and a chance to continue my service with the National Guard. Instead, it had been a challenge. Our new neighbor immediately made it clear that we weren't welcome. He scrutinized our lifestyle, watched us from behind the curtains, and berated us for laughing, playing music, and enjoying cocktails on a Saturday. Everything we did was an invitation for him to antagonize us with criticism and complaints.

One weekend we were visiting family where we used to live, in Las Cruces. It was an ordinary day when the movement on the camera from our home in Santa Fe caught my eye, and what I saw threw my stomach into knots. I could feel in my bones that a personal storm was coming. Two state troopers were knocking on the front door of our house in Sante Fe. I called one of the neighbors, and they told me the troopers had been questioning people about me and my husband and even asking if they thought our daughter was safe.

My mind was reeling from what felt like a bad movie. Two days later I got a call from my colonel. A letter of concern had been sent anonymously, painting a picture of reckless partying and framing our drinking habits as a national security concern. I knew immediately who was behind this smear campaign, and it only got worse from there.

He had also sent a letter to Child Protective Services. The idea that the safety of my child was being questioned made me sick, and she was forced to endure an interview to confirm that she was not in danger. A few more days passed, and we learned that we weren't his only targets. He had apparently harassed others, and the authorities dismissed his complaints and served him with a cease and desist.

But the damage was done, and my secret was out.

I was no longer a *closet* alcoholic. Now, everyone knew.

## THE FOUNDATION OF MY NEW LIFE

I met my husband when I was nineteen. We made some friends who were heavy drinkers and before we knew it had gotten into the habit of drinking every night. When I was in college, I would drink each night and then go to class and to work completely hungover. After graduation I was offered a chance to be an assistant teacher at the university. More than once they had to cancel my class because I was too hungover to teach. The humiliation I felt was terrible, but not terrible enough to make me quit. Instead, I learned to be a functional alcoholic. I made it to work every day and somehow met my deadlines, which validated my belief that I didn't have a problem.

When I got pregnant with my daughter, I stopped drinking, but the relief was short-lived. I was having trouble breastfeeding and was told that sometimes drinking a beer helped the milk come in. That was all the permission I needed. That one beer led me back into the spiral of alcoholism for another eleven years.

My child was never in danger. I drank only in my home and never drove. But when that neighbor finally exposed me, the reality sank in. The roles I cherished were suddenly in jeopardy, and my reputation, family, and everything I held dear was on the line. Yet as the weeks passed, I began to feel an odd sense of calm. I could no longer pretend I didn't have a problem. The harassment from my neighbor ended up being a blessing in disguise, the catalyst to a journey that would change my life.

I arrived at WISH rehab in California riddled in fear that I was going to be one of the many who go to rehab only to return home and start drinking again. Shortly after arriving, they gave me a roommate. She was in heavy detox, and watching it was excruciating. I became upset at this arrangement, and on my descent down the stairs I missed a step and severely injured my ankle. Now I was in rehab *and* on crutches.

Little did I know this injury would lead me to discover a strength and resilience I didn't know I possessed. It was the first step in becoming an athlete, not just in body but in spirit—a fighter who could rise above challenges and take control of her own destiny. Resilience and self-leadership would soon become not just tools for survival but the foundation of my new life.

## IT STARTS WITH YOU

Today, I am fifty years old, three years sober and with a mission to help my clients achieve their highest goals and aspirations. It has been a slow but beautiful unfolding into the person I was meant to be. The mile markers of our lives are all connected, breadcrumbs to follow on our way to becoming the best versions of ourselves. Had I never been traumatized by the neighbor, I may never have gone to rehab. Had I not gone to rehab, I wouldn't be sober. Had my roommate's detox not sent me running down the stairs, I may never have hurt my ankle. Had I not hurt my ankle, I would never have become an amateur athlete!

This journey wasn't just about recovery; it was about transformation. Through my healing I found Jack Canfield's principles of success. Those lessons, combined with the discipline and mindfulness of swimming and cycling, inspired me to create a program for health-conscious professionals and athletes. The Aligned Life Mindset Framework and Mental Toughness Challenge, my signature programs, were created to help regular people achieve performance excellence through the integration of mindset, mental toughness, and mindfulness. It's about challenging individuals to let their bodies be their bosses, cultivate resilience, and ultimately become leaders in their own lives. The Aligned Hearts Relationship and Intimacy Coaching helps people create lasting connections in relationships.

Through this experience, I learned that true leadership begins with leading *yourself*. It's about taking steps forward even when the path ahead feels uncertain. Leadership is about using your experiences to empower others and guide them toward their own breakthroughs. My journey from rehab to becoming an athlete and to now creating the Aligned Life Programs is a testament to the power of resilience, personal growth, and the ability to turn adversity into impact.

It starts within. It starts with a commitment to resilience, the willingness to adapt, and the drive to lean in to the churn!

## RESILIENCE THROUGH PERSONAL GROWTH

Life's challenges can feel like insurmountable roadblocks. For me, resilience has been the bridge between despair and hope. Whether it was my journey of recovering from alcoholism or the arduous process of healing from injury, I've come to understand that resilience isn't about perfection; it's about perseverance, adaptability, and embracing every step of the process.

It became clear that if I wanted to change my life, I had to change my mind. Instead of seeing the three years I spent healing as lost time, I learned to view them as a chapter in my story of resilience. When you can view every step of your journey as a necessary anecdote in your story, recovery becomes less about the limitations of the moment and more about embracing the process of rebuilding.

I learned to take 100 percent responsibility for my circumstances and to view every setback as an opportunity for growth. The more time I spent discovering my own limiting beliefs, thoughts, emotions, and actions, the more I was able to show up authentically and guide others.

No matter what challenges you're facing, know this: Resilience is a skill you can *learn*. Here's how to begin:

1. **Reframe the narrative.** Instead of seeing challenges as barriers, view them as opportunities for growth. Ask yourself, "What can I learn from this?" or, "How can this make me stronger?"

2. **Celebrate small wins.** Progress isn't always linear. Whether it's a day of sobriety, a moment of self-kindness, or a milestone in physical recovery, celebrate it. These small victories are the foundation of resilience.

3. **Lean in to self-awareness.** Spend time reflecting. Practices such as journaling can help you tune in to your inner voice and stay grounded in your journey.

4. **Visualize your future.** Imagine the version of yourself who has overcome today's challenges. Hold on to that vision as a reminder of what you're working toward, even when the road feels long.

5. **Stay flexible and curious.** Life rarely goes according to plan, but that doesn't mean you've failed. Approach setbacks with curiosity: "What's next? How can I adapt?" Flexibility is one of resilience's greatest allies.

Your journey will be filled with twists and turns. Keep going! You're not just surviving; you're building a life that reflects your endless courage and determination. And if you don't feel you have any courage, get inspired by someone else.

## ADAPTING TO LIMITATIONS

The commercial starts and the camera zooms in to a sweat-drenched forehead. It travels down then to laces being tied, and the athlete stands up, poised to launch into a run. The camera follows as her shoes hit the pavement, a rhythm that matches the upbeat music and the cadence of the narrator's voice.

When the lens finally pans out to the athlete's face, it is not a famous track star, but *Sister Madonna Buder, a Roman Catholic nun and the oldest woman ever to finish an Ironman triathlon. Buder began her athletic training at around fifty years old and has completed more than 340 triathlons.* She is ninety years old now and still participating in marathons! When a friend told me Sister Madonna's story, I was instantly inspired.

My ankle injury was proving to be a tough adversary, but if the Iron Nun could do it, so could I! I knew I needed a fitness plan to stay sober, yet walking was excruciating, on land. I decided to try the therapy pool and realized that I *could* walk, so long as it was in water! Five days a week I walked across that pool with my ankle on the ground as it was supposed to be.

After following that routine for a while, I was able to put weight on my ankle on dry land. That experience reinforced the idea that leadership isn't about forcing a single path; it's about finding solutions that align with your current reality.

With a growth mindset, being an athlete isn't about perfection or peak performance; it's about showing up, pushing limits, and listening to your body when you need rest or pivot. It's about thriving in the mindset of "What's next?" rather than getting stuck in *what was.*

Sister Madonna Buder's story and my own can serve as reminders that we are not fixed into any one version of our lives. Whether it's recovering from an injury or starting a new chapter later in life, resilience often begins with a willingness to adapt. Like her, I learned that progress isn't always about following the path we envisioned but about finding new ways to move forward. The lesson is this: No matter your age or circumstance, there is always a way to push forward and redefine what's possible.

# THE POWER OF THE CHURN

Imagine setting out to climb a mountain, only to find the trail blocked by fallen trees. Do you turn back or find another way forward? That process of recalibrating your approach while keeping your destination in sight is what I call the churn. The churn matters because it teaches us flexibility and the value of the journey itself.

For me, the churn became real when I took up cycling in 2023. I started with a gravel bike and short rides, just a few miles at nine to ten miles per hour. I didn't know much about pacing or training, but I had the guidance of a semipro friend who encouraged me to build slowly, adding small amounts of mileage each week to gain endurance. Following his advice, I worked my way up to fifteen miles and then twenty.

My first major pivot came when I bought a road bike. I joined group rides and started pushing my limits. Those moments, even when exhausting, gave me a sense of accomplishment I hadn't felt in years. They also sparked something deeper—a reflection on my past and the activities I'd let slip away. As a kid, I loved biking, but life pulled me away from it. Cycling now, in my late forties, felt like reclaiming a part of myself I'd thought was gone.

But the churn doesn't stop once you're on a roll. My old ankle injury resurfaced, forcing me to slow down and rethink my approach. I returned to basics, cycling shorter distances. Just as I began rebuilding, I overtrained and injured my knee, setting me back again. Frustration could have derailed me, but I leaned in to the churn instead, focusing on listening to my body's needs while adjusting my training again.

The churn has taught me invaluable lessons about adaptability. I've learned that progress isn't about perfection or relentless momentum. It's about finding *new* ways to move forward.

For anyone navigating their own churn, keep your end goal in sight, but stay open to change. The road to success is rarely linear. Embrace the churn, and remember that every phase and pivot of the journey is a vital step in reaching your ultimate potential.

Stay committed to your decisions and goals, and be flexible and open in your actions and approach.

## STEADY ON

Storms are an inevitable part of life. They can come on suddenly. They can uproot what was hidden and reveal what was buried.

In the wake of a storm, the world looks chaotic, but it's also honest. Storms force a reckoning and demand adaptation. Leadership, like life, is shaped in these moments—not in the calm but in the turmoil of the storm.

For me, the storm hit when my neighbor's actions exposed a truth I had hidden for years. It felt as if everything were breaking at once—my reputation, my privacy, and the facade I'd built to shield my struggles with alcohol. I felt uprooted, exposed, and drenched in shame. But when the rain stopped, I realized something profound: The storm didn't just destroy—it cleared the way for me to start anew.

Leadership isn't forged in perfection or unbroken paths; it's built in the moments when you stand amid the wreckage and choose to rebuild. It's the decision to face what the storm has unearthed and use it as a foundation for growth. It's finding strength in vulnerability, clarity in chaos, and courage in recalibration.

So, if you're navigating a personal storm, steady on. It is preparing you, strengthening you, and, if you let it, leading you to the best, healthiest, most authentic version of yourself!

## About Rose

For over twenty years, Rose Barr built a career in accounting, government audit, defense contracting, and business-strategy consulting. Through her expertise in financial analysis, operational efficiency, and strategic problem-solving, she developed a keen understanding of not just businesses but the people behind them—their behaviors, their decision-making processes, and the psychological forces that drive success or lead to burnout.

Her fascination with human behavior, mindset, mental toughness, and mindfulness led her to recognize a deeper pattern: Success in business, fitness, relationships, and personal growth isn't just about strategy; it's about resilience, emotional regulation, and the ability to shift perspectives. This realization propelled her into coaching, mindset work, and performance psychology, where she now specializes in guiding athletes, entrepreneurs, and professionals, especially women, through transformative breakthroughs.

Rose blends deep analytical thinking with mindset mastery, bridging logic and intuition to help clients rewire unproductive patterns and align their actions with their highest potential. Whether coaching through major transitions, optimizing decision-making, or reigniting inner motivation, her approach integrates neuroscience-backed strategies, emotional intelligence, and practical psychology. She goes beyond traditional mindset work, helping clients break through mental barriers, dismantle limiting beliefs, and cultivate lasting resilience.

Passionate about both mental and physical well-being, Rose is an adventurer at heart. When she's not coaching, she can be found exploring the outdoors, camping by a fire, playing cards, and sharing laughter. A dedicated cyclist—both road and mountain biking—she also finds peace and grounding in swimming. Constantly pushing her own boundaries, she lives what she teaches, embracing personal growth, challenge, and adventure at every turn.

If you want more information on her work, Rose can be reached at rosebarr.com. She is on social media at Rose Barr, Aligned Life, and Aligned Hearts.

# CHAPTER 12

# LEAD THE CHARGE, LEAD YOURSELF, LEAD THE WAY

*Navigating the Seasons of Leadership
with Strength and Purpose*

———————

By Katie Schuelke

I
t has been said that a river cuts through rock not because of its power but because of its persistence.

Rivers twist and turn, weaving around jagged rocks and flowing through anything in their way. They are unyielding, purposeful, and relentless in their paths.

But seasons change, and so do rivers. In the summer heat they rush forward. In the dead of winter, they freeze into a strong silence. Come spring, they melt and meander, nurturing the land around them and carrying away what they no longer need.

Each change of season brings a new purpose. Leadership, I have come to learn, is much like the river. It is not static or confined to a single flow. There are moments when it demands urgency, cutting through obstacles with focused precision. At other times it needs quiet reflection so we can determine the right moment to move.

As I reflect on my journey, I see the ebb and flow of my own leadership, shaped by the seasons of my life, the moments that hardened me, the crises that softened me, and the challenges that called for courage and compassion.

Life, in its ever-changing rhythm, shapes, molds, and transforms us into who we need to be to meet each moment that comes our way.

I've been in seasons that propelled me forward and others that slowed me down.

Each season serves a purpose, brings a lesson, and ultimately shows us exactly what we're capable of. We simply need to have the courage to follow the flow, trust the moment, and lead the charge.

## LEAD THE CHARGE

My best friend and I had been inseparable since junior high. We graduated from school together, went to college together, and were even pregnant at the same time. She was my anchor, my sounding board and my partner through good times and bad.

Together with her nine-month-old son, we celebrated my daughter's first birthday. Two weeks later my best friend was dead.

To this day no one is quite sure what happened, and it still feels surreal, even now. When I found out, she was in the hospital, hooked to life support, her brain had shut down, and the doctors had confirmed there was no hope. I couldn't wrap my head around it. How was this possible?

The unimaginable weight of saying goodbye to someone who had shared my life in every meaningful way was a grief I had never known.

As I sat with her, the life support being removed, the speed of her heart went down, and the wall around my heart went up.

After losing her, I withdrew. Personal relationships became too risky. What was the point of opening my heart when life could snatch something away in an instant? So I did the one thing I knew I could do well from behind my wall: I worked. I compartmentalized. I built an internal fortress and threw myself into action.

Here's the paradox of tragedy—it doesn't just take from you. Sometimes it gives. In losing my best friend, I gained my courage. After all, I had come face to face with the harsh reality that life is terribly short. Why not take chances, charge forward, and give it all I had?

When there was a challenge to face, I was the one who stepped forward. I knew now that I could handle the hard things, so when the stakes were high, I became the person who could carry the weight.

Tragedy can gift us with focus. It becomes a fire that drives you and demands you do something with what you've survived.

For me, my friend's death forced me to see that life's fragility isn't something to fear; it's something to honor by showing up fearlessly when it matters most.

My focused determination not only shielded me from heartache and guided me through grief; it pushed me forward in my career.

When you stand in that space of unstoppable drive, others will follow because they see your strength.

They see that you're not moving forward despite the storm; you're moving forward *because* of it.

## LEAD THE CONVERSATION

Leadership often begins with having conversations no one else wants to have. For me, one of those conversations came when I found myself in a delicate situation. The morale of my project team was unraveling, and it was up to me to address it.

I had been tasked with managing a high-stakes project—one unlike anything we'd handled before. The new VP had decided to bring in a contractor, someone she deemed an expert, to guide us. The "expert," however, wasn't just knowledgeable—she was abrasive, rude, and dismissive. Instead of empowering the team with her expertise, she was undermining them. The challenge was, she was a good friend of the VP's.

The tension was palpable. Team members were frustrated, and the stress of an already high-pressure project was pushing people to their limits. I knew something had to change. I didn't have formal authority to address the situation, and taking this issue to her was a risk.

I could have stayed silent. I could have convinced myself it wasn't my place or rationalized that the fallout wasn't my responsibility. But that's not what leaders do. Leadership isn't about rank or title—it's about stepping into the space where change is needed.

The truth is, conflict is inevitable in any setting, especially under stress. The difference between thriving teams and dysfunctional ones isn't the absence of conflict but the ability to navigate it with purpose. This is the heart of healthy conflict—addressing challenges openly, honestly, and constructively.

So I led a conversation.

I scheduled a meeting with the VP, not to criticize her decision but to highlight the dynamics it had created. I explained what the team was experiencing—the stress, the feelings of being undervalued, and the way the contractor's approach was affecting the culture. I approached it from a place of collaboration, not accusation, and I asked what we could do together to improve the situation.

Conversations like this are never easy, but I've learned that the hardest conversations are often the most necessary. When done with empathy and intention, they lead to transformation.

We came up with a plan. The contractor's role was adjusted, and I worked to ensure the team felt heard and valued moving forward. Slowly but surely, morale improved, and so did our results.

The lesson? Healthy conflict is a communication tactic every leader must master. It's not about avoiding tension but engaging with it in a way that builds trust and solves problems. Here's what that requires:

1. **Courage to start the conversation:** People avoid conflict because they fear the outcome, but most fears are rooted in uncertainty, not reality. Change requires the courage to take the first step.

2. **Empathy over accusation:** Approaching the conversation from a place of understanding and curiosity, not blame, is key to defusing any tension. The more curious we are, the more we learn, and the more information we have with which to form a solution.

3. **Clarity and collaboration:** Leading the conversation doesn't mean controlling it—it means creating space for progress.

Can you think of a situation you're in now that is begging for a tough talk? I can tell you from experience that the tension caused by words unspoken is much worse than the temporary discomfort of truth.

By leaning in to healthy conflict, you can transform even the most contentious dynamics into opportunities for growth.

## LEAD YOURSELF

Most of us know what it's like to be stuck in a toxic work environment. You waste most of your Sunday dreading Monday. You walk into work feeling like you're walking the plank, heavy with the knowledge that at some point you're likely to be undermined, mistreated, or disrespected.

I was doing my best to push through the dysfunction, telling myself that I could handle it and that the camaraderie I felt with my team, who had become like family, made it all worth it. I was a pro at compartmentalizing, so day after day I ignored the dread that was creeping in and the urgent pleas from my intuition.

And that's when the room started spinning.

The walls felt as if they were closing in, and as extreme disconcertment set in, so did nausea. I tried to walk but immediately realized that remaining completely immobile was the only way to stop the torturous dizziness that had suddenly taken over. It was vertigo.

It was no longer safe to drive, so I was not able to go into the office. That's when things started clicking.

The more time I spent away from the office, the better I felt.

Once I stepped away from the noise and busyness of that life, I was left with something I had avoided for far too long: my thoughts and feelings. Without the constant distractions, I had to make a choice—confront the truths I'd been ignoring or continue down a path that was making me unwell.

Then COVID hit, and suddenly the office was empty, the chaos of my workdays evaporated, and I was alone. My husband, an essential worker for UPS, was rarely home, and the silence was profound. At first it felt isolating, but over time that calm became a gift. It created the space I needed to begin healing.

I set out on a journey of transformation, focusing on holistic health, functional medicine, and energy work. I stepped away from prescriptions and started to truly nurture my physical health—and in doing so, I unlocked the door to mental and spiritual health as well.

As I healed, I realized that many of us find ourselves carried along a current, and before we know it, we've fallen into the trap of the conformity constraint.

The conformity constraint is a circumstance where our authenticity is inhibited.

This can come from a genuine desire to be accepted. We learn to behave differently in order to fit in or because we have observed or received actual consequences for going against the grain.

The problem is that if we are all conforming, we're not working from our authentic selves, which is ultimately detrimental to the culture and the results. Not only is it hard on people's mental and physical health to spend so many hours a day playing a character rather than being themselves, but you cannot create a high-performing innovative team if people are hesitant to bring their different points of view to the table.

Innovation needs diversity of thought! The most creative ideas are born from a fusion of viewpoints that were grown from individual seeds of authenticity.

Once I was out of the toxic situation, it became clear that one of my authentic needs was that my work had to align with my values and energy. The illness had been a wake-up call, a stark reminder that when your work and life are out of alignment, the cost can be your health and happiness.

I started thinking about what I wanted to add to the business I'd launched in 2015. I knew it had to evolve to reflect the lessons I had learned. Today, I help thought leaders and changemakers unlock the leader within, guiding them to challenge the cultural, corporate, and systemic pressures that keep us trapped in outdated molds.

What I learned is that to be the most powerful leader for others, you must first lead yourself. Create space for reflection so you can hear your own inner voice. Align your actions with your core values so that you're not exhausting yourself in a role you were never meant to play. Invest in your own well-being so you can serve others from a full cup. Most importantly, redefine success on your terms. Step away from societal and cultural expectations long enough to decide what success looks like for you. Leadership isn't about fitting into a mold; it's about challenging it.

Arianna Huffington was quoted as saying that "restore connection" is not just for devices; it's for us too. By choosing to restore your connection to your own values and desires, you pave the way for a life and career that doesn't just work—it thrives.

Sometimes the greatest accomplishment you can achieve as a leader is learning to lead as *yourself.*

## LEAD THE WAY

Rosalynn Carter once said, "A leader takes people where they want to go. A great leader takes people where they don't necessarily want to go, but ought to be."

A title, a corner office and a team of employees to manage is not what makes a leader. A leader is a visionary with the capacity to hold integrity in the face of adversity, courage in the face of change, and empathy in the face of conflict.

A leader does the hard thing if it's the right thing, and usually the character traits that make them valuable to the office are the same ones that make them loved and cherished at home.

Once I had my daughter, I felt a major shift. I knew that I could no longer compartmentalize. I had to dial in a way of being that was authentic regardless of my environment. The qualities my team needed me to have were the same ones my daughter would need me to display at home.

And likewise, my coworkers deserved the same care and patience I extended to my child. When I led the way toward dissolving the line between work and home, between corporate Katie and personal Katie, something extraordinary happened. The people I worked with opened up to me too. I forged connections to my team, and that connection built trust. That trust cultivated a spirit of warm collaboration that ultimately resulted in an ongoing season of success.

Leadership, like the river, is not a fixed state. It adapts to the seasons of life, responding to the changes and challenges that shape us. Whether cutting through obstacles with unwavering determination, slowing down in reflective stillness, or nurturing growth and transformation, it flows in many forms.

As I reflect on my journey, I see that every challenge, every loss, and every moment of courage has carved a path, just as water carves through rock. The flow of leadership is not about perfection; it's about perseverance. It's about showing up, fully present, even when the current feels too strong or the waters too still.

Ultimately, leadership isn't about controlling the flow—it's about embracing it. It's about becoming the force that moves forward, carrying others along and leaving the world a little stronger, a little more hopeful, and a little more inspired in its wake.

## About Katie

Katie Schuelke is a best-selling author, leadership strategist, and the founder and chief rebel officer of Liberated Leader. With over twenty-five years of experience in project management and team leadership, she helps bold, purpose-driven leaders break free from outdated systems, build engaged teams, and lead authentically.

Her maverick perspective on transformation and leadership challenges outdated rules and empowers leaders to create impact on their own terms. With a background in project management, IT integration, and business strategy, Katie has led high-stakes, multimillion-dollar initiatives across industries. Holding a Project Management Professional (PMP) certification and a Six Sigma Greenbelt, she blends structure with agility, strategy with intuition, and discipline with a rebellious streak.

Known for her innate ability to inspire and motivate, Katie is often described as intuitive, insightful, tenacious, and trustworthy—a rebel at heart with a mischievous sense of humor. She believes leadership should be an adventure, not a cage, and equips small-business owners, project managers, and emerging leaders with the power skills they need to influence, inspire, and innovate. A passionate believer in reciprocity and positive change, she is dedicated to helping leaders build confidence, clarity, and authentic influence.

A lifelong learner and fierce advocate for personal growth, Katie is a dedicated wife and mother who's very proud of her daughter, Kennedy—who has grown into her own leader, forging her own path with resilience, determination, and heart. As someone who believes in making adventure as you go, Katie also loves mid-to-late '60s muscle cars because, like great leadership, they are bold, powerful, and unapologetically badass.

One client said of her: "Katie brings a lot of energy, passion, and dedication to her work. Really enjoyable person to be around. Definitely a positive booster to your work culture....She is great to counsel with and talk strategy with. Her depth of knowledge on project management, organizational human dynamics, and level of emotional intelligence make her an asset to organizations and teams."

Learn more at www.liberatedleader.me.